Restoring Sanity

Other Books by Margaret J. Wheatley

Who Do We Choose to Be? Facing Reality, Claiming Leadership, Restoring Sanity

So Far from Home: Lost and Found in Our Brave New World

Walk Out Walk On: A Learning Journey into Communities Daring to Live the Future Now, coauthored with Deborah Frieze

Perseverance

Finding Our Way: Leadership for an Uncertain Time

Turning to One Another: Simple Conversations to Restore Hope to the Future

A Simpler Way, coauthored with Myron Kellner-Rogers

Leadership and the New Science: Discovering Order in a Chaotic World

How Does Raven Know? Entering Sacred World: A Meditative Memoir

Warriors for the Human Spirit: A Songline, A Journey Guided by Voice and Sound

Restoring Sanity

Practices to Awaken Generosity, Creativity, & Kindness in Ourselves and Our Organizations

Margaret J. Wheatley

Berrett–Koehler Publishers, Inc.
a BK Life book

Berrett-Koehler Publishers, Inc.
1333 Broadway, Suite 1000
Oakland, CA 94612-1921
Tel: (510) 817-2277
Fax: (510) 817-2278
www.bkconnection.com

ORDERING INFORMATION
Quantity sales. Special discounts are available on quantity purchases by corporations, associations, and others. For details, contact the "Special Sales Department" at the Berrett-Koehler address above.
Individual sales. Berrett-Koehler publications are available through most bookstores. They can also be ordered directly from Berrett-Koehler: Tel: (800) 929-2929; Fax: (802) 864-7626; www.bkconnection.com.
Orders for college textbook / course adoption use. Please contact Berrett-Koehler:
Tel: (800) 929-2929; Fax: (802) 864-7626.

Distributed to the U.S. trade and internationally by Penguin Random House Publisher Services.

Printed in the United States of America

Berrett-Koehler books are printed on long-lasting acid-free paper. When it is available, we choose paper that has been manufactured by environmentally responsible processes. These may include using trees grown in sustainable forests, incorporating recycled paper, minimizing chlorine in bleaching, or recycling the energy produced at the paper mill.

Library of Congress Cataloging-in-Publication Data

First Edition
30 29 28 27 26 25 24 23 10 9 8 7 6 5 4 3 2 1

Book design: Canace Pulfer
Author photo: Canace Pulfer

Why wouldn't I dedicate a book focused
on awakening the human spirit to all of us,
eight billion spirits and counting?
So I do.

I used to ask, "What's wrong? How can I fix it?"
Then I realized the right question was:
"What's possible and who cares?"

Marvin Weisbord
Author, consultant, OD elder

Contents

Part Two: Practices to Awaken Generosity, Creativity, and Kindness

If you do not do what you cannot do
that is not a problem.
If you do not do what is yours to do,
you are a disaster,
a wasted life.

Sadhguru
Yogi, mystic, visionary

Dear Reader,

I have worked with leaders on all continents (except Antarctica) and at all levels since 1973, and I state with full confidence that leadership has never been more difficult. And it's not our fault. No matter that we've been good and caring leaders in the past, no matter that we've led people in empowering, engaging ways that resulted in meaningful, productive work, we now face external conditions far beyond our control to change. And these external factors are intensifying their impacts at shocking speed.

The perfect storm is here, created by the coalescence of climate and human-created catastrophes, insatiable greed, fear-based self-protection, escalating aggression and conflict, indifference for the well-being of others, and continuing uncertainty. As leaders dedicated to serving the causes and people we treasure, confronted by this unrelenting tsunami, what are we to do? My answer to this is also stated with full confidence: We need to restore sanity by awakening the human spirit. We can only achieve this if we undertake the most challenging and meaningful work of our leader lives: creating Islands of Sanity.

This book offers practices for creating and sustaining these islands. I know that this island mentality is necessary, the last opportunity for sane leadership. To understand this necessity, to bring this time into clear focus, to let clarity inspire and motivate you to embrace the challenge to restore sanity, please read my 2023 book *Who Do We Choose to Be? Facing Reality | Claiming Leadership | Restoring Sanity.* That is the parent text that gave birth to this book of practices.

If there is no sense of rejoicing
and magical practice,
you find yourself simply driving into
the high wall of insanity.

Chögyam Trungpa
Buddhist teacher

Maybe you understand where we are on the pattern of collapse, maybe you need more convincing, maybe you seek greater depth of understanding, maybe you're just curious about my latest work. Whoever you may be, my aspiration is for you to undertake this difficult and meaningful work of creating an Island of Sanity. Please develop a strong foundation in knowing why this work is necessary. This clarity, combined with your faith in people and your dedication to serve, will strengthen you for whatever future we will encounter.

Margaret Wheatley
Sundance Utah, January 2024

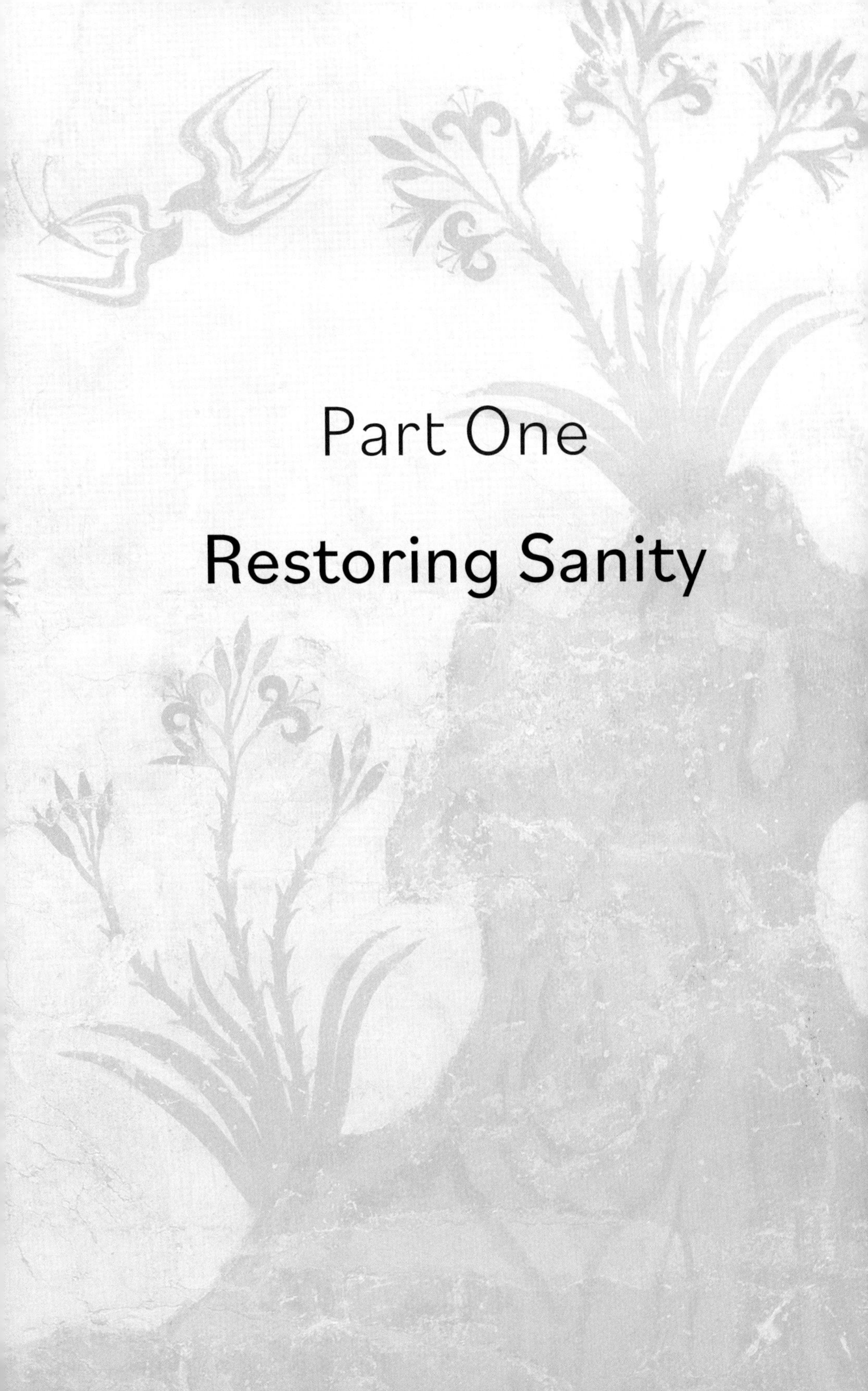

Part One

Restoring Sanity

Part One

Restoring Sanity

It Is a Wondrous Thing

It is a wondrous thing to know each other as humans being fully human.

It is a wondrous thing to be able to restore sanity.

It is a wondrous thing to awaken our human spirits.

It is a wondrous thing to know all humans can be generous, creative, and kind.

It is a wondrous thing to partner with life and Spirit.

It is a wondrous thing to experience uncertainty as inviting rather than frightening.

It is a wondrous thing to create Islands of Sanity—places of possibility and refuge where the human spirit can thrive.

Restoring sanity is joyful work.

May we become intimate with this joy.

1

My Gift to You

Gifts are meant to delight and surprise us. That's why people who care about us offer them to us. This book is my gift to you, filled with perspectives and practices chosen for their power to restore and awaken the human spirit, to enrich our capacity to work well together, to create more goodness and possibility. At this time when lives and possibilities are destroyed by casual destructive decisions, I aspire for us to be sane leaders devoted to restoring and awakening the finest qualities of being human—our generosity, creativity, and kindness. We will not change the world, but we can create Islands of Sanity where our human spirits come alive and we contribute in ways that make more possible.

What becomes possible when we dedicate ourselves to using everything within our power to awaken the human spirit? We humans, with our wondrous capacities for generosity, creativity, and kindness. We humans, with our wondrous capacities buried by oppression, venality, and indifference. We humans, with our wondrous capacities forgotten or never known, or told we don't have them.

What an insane world this is, to be destroying these qualities when they are most needed! For whatever future awaits us, we need human beings being fully human.

Restoring sanity is very hard work—and it's the only work worth doing. Who knows if we'll succeed, but the joy is in the trying. The meaning is in moments when we know we did something good—we supported a person, we brought possibilities into form, we strengthened our community, we kept going against all odds.

Shall we do this work to restore sanity? As President Teddy Roosevelt enjoined us: "Do what you can, where you are, with what you have." Let's do what we can. To choose otherwise is truly insane—we'd be contributing to the continuing destruction of the human spirit. What greater crime is there?

Nothing here is easy to do—but nothing is easy these days. Yet every moment when a person or group discovers their potential and contributes generosity, creativity, and kindness, this is a joyful moment, a moment we remember, a moment whose meaning will live inside us always.

What a bold and beautiful experiment—to explore the reaches of the human spirit in this time when so little feels sacred, not even humans. May we choose to be those who restore sanity, awaken our human spirits, and experience the wonders of who we humans can be, no matter what is happening in the external world.

We can put our whole heart into whatever we do; but if we freeze our attitude into for or against, we're setting ourselves up for stress. Instead, we could just go forward with curiosity, wondering where this experiment will lead. This kind of open-ended inquisitiveness captures the spirit of enthusiasm, or heroic perseverance.

Pema Chödrön
Buddhist teacher

2

What Would It Be Like?

What would it be like to work together again in creative and generous ways? What would it be like to expect kindness and generosity? What would it be like to want to contribute as fully as possible, to feel welcomed and appreciated for my contribution?

What would it be like to be curious about who you're with rather than judging or fearing them? What would it be like to engage together exploring possibilities rather than withdrawing in conflict or disagreement? What would it be like to be working well together?

It is still possible to create the conditions for people to engage together for work they care about. But this work requires devotion, discipline, and faith. It requires sane leaders who have unshakable confidence that people can be generous, creative, and kind. It requires setting ourselves apart as an Island of Sanity.

The dynamics of fear and denial have taken hold and cannot be changed at the macro level. If we know our human spirits, if we know what people are capable of, if we remember working well together, we will have the motivation to separate ourselves from this oppressive and destructive culture. We will focus our energy and aspirations to create Islands of Sanity.

If you're curious about sane leadership, if you're curious about what it takes to awaken people's innate generosity, creativity, and kindness, please stay with me.

These things, these things were here
and but the beholder
Wanting.

Gerard Manley Hopkins
Poet

3

What Is the Human Spirit?

The human spirit exists beyond the physical realm of mind and body. The human spirit exists in a dimension never revealed by the five senses. When freed from the physical, the human spirit soars with Creation, the Sacred, God, the Great Mystery. The human spirit is boundless when liberated from fear and self-preservation.

We human spirits want to learn and grow. When held in community, no longer frightened and alone, we eagerly step forward. We want to contribute. We want to strengthen our community. We want to engage together in making sense and solving problems.

No longer imprisoned by fear and isolation, the human spirit is a wondrous source of generosity, creativity, and kindness.

My continuing passion would be . . . to part a curtain,
that invisible shadow that falls between people,
the veil of indifference to each other's presence,
each other's wonder,
each other's human plight.

Eudora Welty
Writer

4

To Restore and Awaken

We can only restore what's already present. We can only awaken what's been asleep.

As we aspire to restore sanity and awaken generosity, creativity, and kindness in ourselves and in our organizations, we do not have to create, fill in the gaps, motivate, or train for these qualities. Humans innately possess these qualities by virtue of being human.

We know these qualities in ourselves. Our work is to know, with unshakable confidence, that these are human, not personal, qualities. Just like me, everyone wants to be generous, creative, and kind.

A terrible desertification has occurred in too many organizations, barren landscapes now devoid of life and human potential. Leadership has created these by striving for obedience rather than contribution, choosing greed and power rather than inclusion and engagement. Everywhere now we see the consequences of denying, ignoring, and suppressing the human spirit.

Can we envision ourselves as devoted explorers of these deserts, knowing there are deep underground wells of possibility? Can we use our power and influence to create sanctuaries to awaken and restore our finest human qualities? Can we be those who know what's gone underground and, through our actions, nourish and revive these wellsprings of human potential?

Ours is not the task of fixing
the entire world all at once,
but of stretching out to mend
the part of the world that is within our reach.
Any small, calm thing that
one soul can do to help another soul,
to assist some portion of this poor suffering world,
will help immensely.

Clarissa Pinkola Estés
Writer

5

Islands of Sanity

An Island of Sanity is a gift of possibility and refuge. It is a true island because it sets itself apart from the destructive dynamics, policies, and behaviors that are afflicting people on the mainland.

It needs to be an island because there is no other way to preserve and protect our best human qualities. We are not seeking sanctuary; we are seeking contribution. We are magnetized by the island's offerings—the possibility of working together in harmonious relationships to accomplish meaningful work.

This current culture, with people locked down in fear and self-protection, is destroying our relationships, our work, and our future. It is easier to withdraw than to step forward. It is safer to protect oneself than to be visible. This is the harsh reality that defines the need for Islands of Sanity.

We do not withdraw. We are not seeking self-protection. We commit to creating a community where generosity, creativity, and kindness are the norm—what we expect from each other and easily offer in return.

We realize that the current culture cannot create the conditions for these behaviors. Although they are natural to the human spirit, this culture has normalized greed, aggression, and life-destroying behaviors. In this ruthless environment, what's needed is not individual acts of heroism, but island communities where sanity prevails.

What is this island? It's rarely a physical form. It's an orientation, an aspiration, a commitment born from our deepest motivation to contribute to this time in meaningful and purposeful ways. We realize we can no longer participate in the general culture because its dynamics are overpowering us. Even though we want to be generous, creative, and kind, we too often find ourselves caught in aggression and fear. We notice that, although we know better and have behaved better, we're now becoming distrustful, angry, fearful—just like everybody else.

How do we stop this downward trend of bad behaviors? We need to create a boundary, a protective way of being that reduces the impact of these negative forces. We need to set ourselves apart and claim who we choose to be. We choose to be *Warriors for the Human Spirit,* people dedicated to creating the conditions for more people to realize their best human qualities. And for those who will never be released from their fear and anger, we want to be generous and kind.

We cannot do this alone. We need to gather together with others who are motivated by the same sense of call. We develop an island mentality not to exclude but to increase our capacity to serve. An Island of Sanity takes form from our intentions and aspirations. It develops strength and capacity as we work hard, struggle, stay together, figure things out, fail, succeed, learn, forgive, laugh, persevere.

It is pure gift to dedicate ourselves to creating these sanctuaries of possibility. May joy be our familiar companion.

The world speaks everything to us.
It is our only friend.

William Stafford
Poet

6

What Is Sanity?

What is sanity? Not in the psychological sense, but in our day-to-day lives, where *crazy* has become the most popular adjective to describe events, comments, decisions, even fun experiences. What is sanity? Is it a standard of conduct? Is it common sense? Is it rational behavior?

Yes, and so much more. Sanity is an honest relationship with reality. Sanity is seeing clearly, free of our filters, judgments, biases. When we see what's going on, then we can discern what actions might be useful. Sanity creates possibilities.

Sanity creates possibility because we see more clearly. We work with what's here, not what we want or hope is here, but what is truly present. One of my spiritual teachers said repeatedly, "You must work with circumstances."

Sanity creates the possibility for wiser actions. When fantasies fade, when hopes and fears no longer obscure our vision, we see what's needed and discern what's possible. We choose our actions from consciousness, not fear. Even if our actions fail, we are more awake, more discerning, more fully human. We can persevere and meet our challenges with greater confidence.

Virtues, for Aristotle, were character traits or psychological dispositions specific to humans, giving us the capacity to relate well to any situation. Rational behavior was a distinctively human quality, not known in animals. Using reason was a virtuous act.

Native Americans did healing practices for the colonizers who broke their treaties with Indigenous tribes. They knew that such people must be insane because they were not in touch with reality. And so they prayed for those truly crazy people.

I am determined
to cultivate only thoughts
that increase trust and love

To use my hands to perform only deeds
that build community

To speak only words of harmony and aid.

Thich Nhat Hanh
Buddhist teacher

7

Sane Leadership

Sane leadership is the unshakable confidence that people can be generous, creative, and kind. The leader's role is to create the conditions for these qualities to be evoked and utilized to accomplish good work.

Among so many fine human qualities, why are these three—generosity, creativity, kindness—singled out as the work of sane leadership? Why not intelligence, courage, love? Of course other qualities are important, but these three are essential to develop trustworthy relationships free of judgments and biases, and to use everyone's talents and perspectives in solving problems they care about. While these qualities are innate in people, it takes certain conditions to evoke them.

If we're better off doing it alone or excluding certain people, there's no need for generosity, creativity, and kindness. Competition and aggression will do just fine.

Sane leadership recognizes these gifts of being fully human. Sanity is recognizing them as real. Leadership is devoting ourselves to creating the conditions so people can manifest them in service to genuine needs and problems.

Because they trust themselves,
they have no need to convince others by deception.
Because their confidence has never wavered,
they are not afraid of anyone.

Chögyam Trungpa
Buddhist teacher

8

Unshakable Confidence

Sane leadership is the unshakable confidence that people can be generous, creative, and kind. Yet to develop unshakable confidence, we need to be grounded in faith, not casual beliefs.

Faith and beliefs are completely different. Beliefs are easy to acquire—so many folks out there are eager to tell us what to believe. We believe what we are told rather than experiencing things directly. Beliefs lack staying power—they come and go, and as they waiver, so do we. If we're motivated by beliefs, not faith, we'll give up when people disappoint us. We may have had a few revelatory moments of witnessing people's capacities, but these vanish with the next disappointment. We lose confidence in people and ourselves. What was I thinking? Why did I ever believe this was possible?

To acquire faith in the human spirit, we need direct experience working with people. Yet our experiences are filtered by beliefs, biases, opinions—we can't help but use interpretive lenses. So we need to train our perception to see more clearly, without our filters. And we need to create and engage in practices that give us direct experience with people's best qualities. Practice makes perfect. Practice makes faith. As our faith deepens, so too does our confidence in people and ourselves to do this work.

Faith in human nature is the ground of being for a sane leader. Without it, we won't keep trying. We won't stay. We'll pick up our exhausted selves and go in search of an easier life. With faith in people, we will stay and keep trying. We will persevere.

When we trust ourselves to not withdraw, when we realize that giving up is not an option, our confidence has become unshakable.

Note: Among the practices in Part Two, there are three focused on faith in people. It's important to do them as they appear, but they are "Surprised by the Human Spirit"; "Do We Share a Faith in the Human Spirit?"; and "Faith as an Antidote to Fear."

This being human is a guest house.

Every morning is a new arrival.

A joy, a depression, a meanness,

some momentary awareness comes as an unexpected visitor.

Welcome and entertain them all! . . .

Treat each guest honorably. . . .

The dark thought, the shame, the malice,

meet them at the door laughing, and invite them in.

Be grateful for whoever comes,

because each has been sent as a guide from beyond.

Molana Jalal ad-Din Rumi
Poet

9

How Do We Humans Change?

How do we humans change? Lately we seem very confused. We assume we have to learn *about* something and become good at it before we practice it, that we have to change ourselves before we set out to change anything. But this is not how change happens.

We change from acting and learning from our actions. We act, learn, and discover what works. Most of us know this is the best process, but we don't do it. We have no time to learn—we just keep digging ourselves deeper into the hole of ignorance and failure.

Direct experience, trying things, is how we develop confidence in our choice of actions. Everything else—beliefs, opinions, theories, practices—came to us from another source. They were told to us and we believed them. Yet if we haven't experienced something directly, outside sources won't change us. We are changed by conscious exploration of our lived experience.

We don't need to perfect ourselves before we commit to the path of sane leadership. We need to be curious practitioners, eager to learn from our experiences. We conduct lots of experiments so we can quickly learn what works to awaken people's generosity, creativity, and kindness. From our brave and conscious actions, from both success and failure, we develop unshakable confidence. Our faith in people grows stronger, and we do too as leaders for this time.

Again and again
some people in the crowd wake up.
They have no ground in the crowd
and they emerge according to broader laws.
They carry strange customs with them,
and demand room for bold gestures.

The future speaks ruthlessly through them.

Rainer Maria Rilke
Poet

10

Awakening Generosity, Creativity, and Kindness

What is the meaning of these very familiar words? Here are a few ways of thinking about each of them that may provoke or inspire you.

Generosity is offering something we value to a person or situation we also value. This is altruism, not reciprocity. We want to extend ourselves or offer something to another. Generosity is a willingness to give without needing to receive. The ultimate generosity is offering something without calling attention to the gift or the giver, and not needing to be thanked. This is why it's named "ultimate"—it's very hard. (By the way, this doesn't apply to what we need to teach our children, who seem quite good at ignoring people's generosity.)

Generosity is born from a relationship we want to support and strengthen. We've become aware of others—what they might need, how we might support them, what will give them pleasure.

If we feel we're sacrificing something to give it to another, we're acting from self-protection, not generosity. We give the gift begrudgingly; we feel we're losing something; we don't really want to give it.

In Buddhism, generosity is the fundamental virtue—without it there can be no ethics, patience, discipline, or perseverance. There are different levels of gifts: most basic is material things, then teachings to help relieve another's suffering, and then fearlessness, the greatest gift we can give to each other.

Kindness too is an offering to others, a way of extending yourself that asks nothing in return. It is kind to be present. It is kind to be open and curious. It is kind to be respectful. It is a great kindness to keep our judgments, biases, and opinions to ourselves, to refrain from inserting them into the work or allowing them to distort our relationships. And we are being kind to ourselves when we commit to clearing our filters. Others benefit, but so do we—life gets much more enjoyable and easeful.

Huston Smith, the superb student of the world's great religions, was asked in an interview with Bill Moyers in 1996 to name what was common among the many faiths he had studied. Smith replied: It sounds a bit simplistic, but they're all saying, Could you just be a little kinder to one another?

Creativity is a natural part of being human. We always seek to notice, make sense, and share with our community. The American poet Mary Oliver said it perfectly: "Instructions for living a life: Pay attention. Be astonished. Tell about it."

We have been creative for as long as our species has existed, and before *Homo sapiens*, earlier hominids were astonishingly kind and creative. With hundreds of thousands of years of expression, we need to notice that, in our time, creativity has been relegated to only a few "artists." The rest of us dull ones need to be trained to be creative. What a tragic waste of humans being human!

The work of the bark painter, or artist,
whatever the medium,
is only partly expressed in the physical creations of
their music, painting, dancing or whatever they use
to give form to their work.

The important thing for them
is the direct way they convey
through the sense of beauty
to the very interior nature of others.

They impart to others and cultivate in them
their own joyous appreciation of
the symmetrical,
the harmonious,
the beautiful and
all that seems most elevating in life.

Cyril Havecker
Warramunga clan, Australia

Historically in many cultures, arts flourish as social and physical conditions deteriorate. Artists express their calls of warning. They want us to remember who we are as conditions threaten to destroy the human spirit. We still treasure their art, temples, and spiritual teachings. (Confucius's teachings and Sun Tzu's *Art of War* were developed during China's Warring States period ~421–222 BCE.)

Creativity also emerges when there's no way out. The Tibetan teacher Chögyam Trungpa noted: "Everything gets clear when you're cornered." Dead ends, unsolvable problems, desperate situations—when we're about to give up, a spark lights in a person or group and a way opens. This is miraculous and predictable—we are naturally creative, especially in the most difficult circumstances.

In ancient cultures—and still today in the few cultures untouched by contact with us—there was no concept of "art." There was no distinction between living and telling about it. Experiences of life were conveyed in many forms, in cave paintings, petroglyphs, pottery, carvings. When we view remnants of ancient cultures today, sometimes we feel these ancestral peoples are still with us, sharing their story.

And still today, in Indigenous rituals, art comes alive as people dance, drum, and chant. Drums and flutes summon ancestors, protectors, and totems. Bodies are painted with intricate patterns and their regalia (clothing) are works of art—beads, bones, jewels, and feathers woven into astonishing tapestries of color and meaning that stop the mind with their beauty and energy.

I should like to think that
[prehistoric man's] first invention,
the first condition for his survival,
was a sense of humor.

André Leroi-Gourhan
Paleoanthropologist

11

What Does It Mean to Be Human?

"What does it mean to be human?" is the question of our time as we deal with AI (artificial intelligence) and omnipresent displays of barbaric human behavior.

Every spiritual tradition and every science (Western, Eastern, Yogic, Indigenous) has sought answers to the questions: Why are we here? What is the meaning of life? How does everything work? How do we work with everything? We've always needed to know how to live as humans in relationship with our lands, our gods, all living beings, and dimensions beyond the physical.

Today, in this brave new world, we need to ask a more fundamental question: Who are we?

We don't know who we are or what to expect from each other. We can't understand the world we created or our place in it. We see horrific behaviors destroying human lives and human potential. We see greed and self-interest destroying the planet. Before we can ask existential questions of "why?" we need to answer "who?"

As neither the enjoyment nor the capacity
of producing musical notes
are faculties of the least use to man
in reference to his daily habits of life,
they must be ranked amongst the most mysterious
with which he is endowed.

Charles Darwin
Naturalist

A Neurobiological Explanation of Human

It is essential but woefully insufficient to understand how we humans work at the physical level of mind and body. Neurobiologists offer invaluable insights and explanations of the human animal. But they are confused and ignorant of us as conscious, self-aware human beings.

The distinction between human animals and human beings is essential. It is essential to know how the human brain evolved from instinctive survival mechanisms to superb expressions of creativity and compassion. The brain works as interdependent neuronal networks communicating among many functional areas. The oldest capacities of the human brain assured survival. Today, whenever we feel threatened, we automatically revert back to fearful reptiles urgently struggling to survive. In this Age of Threat, most people are locked into this primitive brain.

But the human species evolved with extraordinary frontal lobes, brains that gave rise to minds that think, imagine, remember, envision, create, love, dance, and celebrate being alive. Beautiful human minds that can continue to evolve, becoming more conscious, transcending instincts and autonomic reactions. Wondrous potential, if we use our awareness.

Neurobiologists will never explain consciousness, thought, generosity, courage, love, or any other magnificent human capacity. They're looking in the wrong place—they want physical explanations and utilitarian evolutionary reasons for these most sublime and reliable expressions of what it means to be human. They would do well to stop using the physical to understand what's beyond the physical, but that will never happen. We, however, can put aside their debasing explanations and learn from those who, for countless millennia, have understood and partnered with life and Spirit, receiving abundant gifts of grace from the Great Mystery.

You mustn't be frightened
if a sadness rises in front of you,
larger than any you have ever seen;
if an anxiety, like light and cloud-shadows,
moves over your hands and
over everything you do.
You must realize that something is happening to you,
that life has not forgotten you,
that it holds you in its hand and
will not let you fall.

Rainer Maria Rilke
Poet

Beyond the Physical

All human cultures except the current Western scientific materialistic one understand that life works in many more dimensions than the physical. I hope you've learned this from your own direct experience.

Synchronicities are an easy example of what's going on beyond the physical—a common experience of getting the information you need, or running into the person you wanted to meet, at just the right moment. We've all experienced these, but to what do we attribute their cause? We glibly say, "There are no coincidences," but then what? Who or what creates synchronicities?

I don't need an answer to this question. When synchronicities appear, I use that as a definitive measure that I'm doing my right work. I feel visible and supported beyond my human friends. I acknowledge the gift and get back to my work with renewed vigor and commitment.

But it is the spirit in a person,
the breath of the Almighty,
that gives understanding.

Job 32:8 NCV

Is It Really So Mysterious?

Many times I've heard spiritual teachers and mystics explain that what we call "a miracle" is simply observing one who knows how to work with physical reality, with the basic elements of space, air, water, fire, and earth. And all spiritual and cultural traditions teach how to access and be grateful for experiences with guardian angels, spirits, ancestors. These experiences, told in all faiths in all times, are dismissed as primitive and superstitious by Western scientists, but this is their problem. Can we trust the stories we've heard and the experiences we've had that will never be explained by petty scientific explanations?

What's your experience of sensing, knowing things ahead of time, intuition, knowing when to contact someone? What experiences have you had where the most elegant solution—the simplest—is to give credit to forces, energies, beings beyond the physical realm?

What does it mean to be human?

Are we more than our physical selves?

What gives life meaning?

The simplest way to answer these questions is to understand ourselves.

What Does It Mean to Be You?

Each of us is the best-case example of what it means to be human. We don't have to do research or be informed by others' descriptions. We just need to know ourselves better. (More generalized explanations do help us understand that our experience is not unique to us—and this realization is a big relief. We're human, not some awful anomaly!)

Practice

Know Thyself

You are your best teacher to not only understand yourself, but to then generalize to how most people experience their lives. With these insights into our shared human experience, it becomes easy to want to work to restore sanity.

1. If you experience generosity, creativity, and kindness in yourself

- What situations, moments, and people evoke these behaviors in you?
- When is it easiest to be generous? Creative? Kind?
- How do you feel about yourself at these times?
- Do you feel these are innate or learned qualities?

2. Think of two or three experiences that were most meaningful to you

- What made them meaningful? Be specific; recall details.
- From these memories, what is your personal definition of *meaningful*?

3. At the end of your life

- What will you look back on as most valued?
- What are you likely to regret or wish you had done differently?
- With this clarity, can you name what you most value?
- With this clarity, will you change your behavior now?

4. Now call to mind the eight billion humans here with you on Earth.

- Can you imagine that nearly every person in this great swell of humanity is more like you than not?
- Can you realize that, "just like me," they too are generous, creative, and kind—or want to be?

Our life circumstances are so different, but even in the worst external circumstances, the human spirit is very hard to extinguish.

If we could read the secret history
of our enemies we would like to punish,
we would find in each life
a sorrow and suffering
enough to disarm all our hostility.

Henry Wadsworth Longfellow
Writer, poet

Practice
Suffering Strangers

This is a simple practice that, when done regularly, opens your heart as wide as the world.

Whenever you see a photo of people who look foreign, different, in terrible circumstances, suffering greatly, take a moment to connect with them. Don't turn away—turn toward them. Make eye contact with them. Develop a momentary relationship, a witnessing of them. Remind yourself that they're just like you. This only takes a moment. Let it become a habit. Whatever your first emotions—sorrow, anger, grief, outrage—as you connect with no-longer-strangers, your first hot reactions will gentle into the coolness of compassion. You will be with them rather than grieving from afar. And compassion soothes us all.

Note: There is another practice, "Just Like Me" (Chapter 20), to use in moments of personal difficulties. This practice grounds your personal suffering in the human experience and thus transforms it. Just like me, how many millions of people are suffering in the same identical way at this very moment?

Humans have a responsibility to their own time,
not as if they could seem to stand outside it
and donate various spiritual and material benefits
to it from a position of compassionate distance.

Humans have a responsibility to find themselves
where they are, in their own proper time and place,
in the history to which they belong and
to which they must inevitably contribute
either their response or their evasions,
either truth and act,
or mere slogan and gesture.

Thomas Merton
Catholic monk, writer, activist

12

Warriors for the Human Spirit

As a sane leader, I invite you to consider an even more noble role for yourself, that of Warrior for the Human Spirit. This is not a casual upgrade. At certain moments in history, when something of great value has needed protecting, a small group of people have arisen to protect and defend what is valued from threats of aggression, corrosion, and loss. Many times, in many places, warriors have arisen to protect wealth, land, and power using weapons of war. But there are countless examples of people who have done all they could to protect people, community, and places under grave threat with peaceful, nonviolent means. Warriors for the Human Spirit join this tradition of peaceful warriors, armed with only two "weapons," compassion and insight.

Warriors are always few in number, perhaps because others realize how much will be asked of them, perhaps because they need to focus on protecting self and family, perhaps because they're unwilling to forgo comforts and take on risks, perhaps because they fail to see that their time in history calls for selfless service.

Historian Sir John Glubb, from careful study of thirteen civilizations at the end of their life cycle, defined the warriors who arise: "While despair might permeate the greater part of the nation, others achieved a new realization of the fact that only readiness for self-sacrifice could enable a community to survive. Some of the greatest saints in history lived in times of national decadence, raising the banner of duty and service against the flood of depravity and despair."

What's your response to this description of a historic role? Does it attract your interest? Or do you not relate to it? Perhaps you don't believe we're in collapse. See how you respond to this description:

> Frivolity, aestheticism, hedonism, cynicism, pessimism, narcissism, consumerism, materialism, nihilism, fatalism, fanaticism and other negative behaviors and attitudes suffuse the population. Politics is increasingly corrupt, life increasingly unjust. A cabal of insiders accrues wealth and power at the expense of the citizenry, fostering a fatal opposition of interests between haves and have nots. The majority lives for bread and circuses; worships celebrities instead of divinities ... throws off social and moral restraints, especially on sexuality; shirks duties but insists on entitlements.

This is not a description from today's news of our 21st-century world. It's from William Ophuls's book *Immoderate Greatness: Why Civilizations Fail* (CreateSpace, 2012). Ophuls describes the behaviors of all complex civilizations in their last stage, the end of their power and glory, the Age of Decadence that precedes collapse. No matter the culture, geographic location, religion, or who's in power, all civilizations decline in identical ways, a very predictable pattern of collapse.

Global civilization is in this last stage, so we need to declare ourselves. We can deny where we are, or we can choose to be leaders who recognize the irreparable harm being done to people and planet. We can be leaders who resolve to put service over self, who learn to stand steadfast in crises and failures. We can be sane leaders, devoted to creating the conditions for people to be generous, creative, and kind.

As Warriors for the Human Spirit, we do everything we can to protect, defend, and preserve the human spirit. We measure our work's success on how valiantly we strove to make more goodness possible in every situation, not on whether we created lasting societal change. We are determined to do our best to stay, to persevere so that we may awaken the greatest resource of all, human beings being fully human.

We take our place in the history of our time, standing on the shoulders of countless warriors who have gone before. It's just our turn.

Note: I have written this as an enticement—everything I do is dedicated to training leaders, activists, and citizens as Warriors for the Human Spirit. If I've aroused your curiosity, my website has an abundance of resources for learning more about this role and the path of training that develops our ability to be the presence of insight and compassion. To learn in greater depth about our culture's last stage, how we got here, and how to respond, please read my book *Who Do We Choose to Be: Facing Reality, Claiming Leadership, Restoring Sanity*, second edition (Oakland, CA: Berrett-Koehler, 2023).

Warriors for the Human Spirit are
awake human beings who have chosen not to flee.
They abide.
They serve as beacons of an ancient story that tells of
the goodness, generosity, and creativity of humanity.
You will know them by their compassionate presence.
You can identify them by their cheerfulness.
When asked how they do it, they will tell you about
discipline, dedication, and the need for community.

A Warrior in training

Part Two

Practices to Awaken Generosity, Creativity, and Kindness

Part Two

Practices to Awaken Generosity, Creativity, and Kindness

13

Discovering Your Leadership

We don't need to search in books or do research to learn who we humans are. We can understand our species through ourselves. As we recall how we've responded in our finest moments, we realize what's possible in all humans with very few exceptions. Just like me, people can be trusted to be generous, creative, and kind in response to challenging situations.

Humans can be quite wonderful, and there's a direct correlation between our discovery of human potential and our desire to use our leadership to bring out the best in people. As our faith in the human spirit deepens, so too does our commitment to create the conditions for more people to discover the wisdom and wealth they possess innately. We willingly take on the role of a Warrior for the Human Spirit.

One of the easiest and most dependable ways for people to discover these qualities in themselves is at work. (I know, I know...it may be hard to remember this given current behaviors.) This is the leader's role—to structure work and sponsor practices that evoke people's innate generosity, creativity, and kindness. As you grow in this role, your faith deepens and your confidence strengthens from witnessing the results of good practices and wise actions. It's a powerful, predictable cycle:

— Your faith in people strengthens from your direct experience. As you develop skills in creating and sponsoring these practices, the boundaries of possibility expand and you become confident that people can take on greater challenges.

— Your faith becomes a wellspring of energy that empowers you to take on the ultimate challenge of creating a place of possibility and sanctuary—an Island of Sanity.

— Your faith in people deepens with experience and nourishes your will and motivation to persevere, to keep going no matter what.

— And then your faith blossoms into meaning and joy as you realize that, even in the worst circumstances, humans can be generous, creative, and kind.

14

Why These Practices?

I chose these practices with great care. They work well to create conditions for people to manifest their best qualities, contributing to resolving issues they care about. They only succeed because of diversity, equality, and inclusion—not as policies but as the only sane means to make sense of complexity and build teams focused on what's possible, not who's here.

I've had many years of experience with each of these practices. Here's a brief description of them. They're organized to provide answers to these key questions:

What does it mean to be human?
We know the human spirit by knowing ourselves. As we reflect on our own experiences, we develop clarity about what it means to be human. The first practices illuminate your personal experiences with generosity, creativity, and kindness. From those experiences, how do you define meaningful work? The last practice asks you to contemplate your personal description of a well-lived life. Now, what will you choose to do with this clarity?

How can personal clarity direct and inspire your leadership?
It is not a casual decision to be a leader dedicated to serving the human spirit, especially as destructive dynamics beyond our control continue to intensify. To assess your current strength as a leader, it's important to notice trends: How have you been changed, for good and ill, during

the past few years? And what will your future leadership be like if you continue unawares? Going forward, if you consciously choose this path of sane leadership, what experiences have given you faith in people? When have you been surprised by the human spirit?

How do we become an Island of Sanity?

Now that you've accepted your role, how do you magnetize people who will commit to creating a place of possibility and sanctuary? Do we really need to be an island? How do we create coherence at the core—a strong identity based on our shared faith in people? Once formed, how do we sustain and nourish our island identity to withstand the forces of storms and erosion?

How do we design practices that awaken generosity, creativity, and kindness?

Here I offer a "pattern language"—design principles that can be trusted to awaken these inherent qualities. As a pattern language, these principles are not human inventions. They draw from life's ways of creating order, balance, and harmony. Working with life's natural dynamics, more becomes possible than with human-invented group processes.

How do we shift from reaction to response?

We don't see clearly. Our vision is obscured by filters, biases, judgments, habits. We get triggered and complicate the situation with our emotional reactions. If we want to see clearly, we commit to clearing our filters, to seeing with new eyes. The first practice opens our perception to new information—we perceive what's new and different in places and people we think we know well. The second practice shifts us from reaction to response, from instant emotions to conscious actions. We learn to clear our filters—projections, biases, judgments—that habitually trigger us. But when we can't stop obsessing about what triggered us, there's a practice for understanding the needs of all involved and developing a response that serves those multiple needs.

What do we do when something goes wrong?
In current culture, we go from crisis to crisis, overwhelmed, exhausted, and incredulous at their frequency. When our Island of Sanity is confronted by a small crisis or a massive failure, it is suicidal to deny, avoid, or hope things will get better on their own. Every crisis is an opportunity to learn in ways that make us smarter and strengthen relationships. Whatever the problem, community is the answer. Two practices are given for dealing with disturbances and crises both real and rumored. And when something truly goes wrong, when we must learn or face continuing failure, two processes for in-depth learning are detailed. Each depends on diversity and inclusion to understand what happened. Each develops greater intelligence and enthusiasm to apply our learnings. Each restores sanity.

What do we do when the road gets hard?
Staying together in the midst of these toxic and turbulent seas is extremely challenging. Staying grounded in our faith when things are falling apart and when outsiders attack us has become a predictable trial by fire. Here are specific practices for using faith as an antidote to fear, for using personal difficulties to connect with the human experience, for dealing with challenges and attacks on your leadership. Lastly, to strengthen you for the long term and to create ever-greater capacity in you to stay sane, I offer two different practices for contemplation and for meditation.

May these practices serve you well as a Warrior for the Human Spirit creating Islands of Sanity, where the finest human qualities will be strengthened for the work that is ours to do, no matter what is happening in the external world.

15

Leading an Island of Sanity

Sane leadership is the unshakable confidence that people can be generous, creative, and kind. The leader's role is to create the conditions for these qualities to be evoked and utilized to accomplish good work.

Practice

How Have You Been Changed as a Leader?

As we do our work and live our lives in this current culture, it's impossible to not be affected by it. We don't want to be short-tempered or impatient, but we are. We don't want to strike out in anger, but we do. We don't want to withdraw and disappear, but we are often tempted. The only way to free ourselves from these negative effects is to become aware of them. Only then can we engage in practices to free ourselves from these dominating negative influences.

Personal Trend Analysis

Why do this: This mini-trend analysis helps you notice how you're doing, how you've changed, and how you're meeting increasing challenges.

How to do this: Please spend time with these eight questions; don't rush or give glib answers. It would be good to contemplate these with someone who cares about you.

1. In the past few years, how have you changed as a leader? Look back and recall a significant leadership moment in the past. Now recall a very recent one. How would you describe yourself then and now? What's changed? What's held constant?

2. Have you become more patient or less? Are you a better listener or not?

3. Have you become more trusting or less trusting of your staff?

4. What keeps you up at night—is this different than in the past?

5. Is your work still meaningful? If yes, what gives it meaning? If not, what's changed?

6. Name the emotions, good and bad, you feel most frequently now. Have you developed healthy ways to deal with them? Or are you coping, treading water? Or are you being dragged under by them?

7. With this understanding of where you are now, where do you think you'll be in another six months or in a year?

8. Thank yourself for being brave enough to do this assessment. Do not feel discouraged—we've all been changed in disheartening ways. Instead, use your clarity as motivation for the work ahead.

Practice

Surprised by the Human Spirit

Why do this: Sane leaders have unshakable confidence that people can be generous, creative, and kind. How did you develop this confidence? Was it through direct experiences with people? Use this practice to recall those moments and events.

How to do this: Remember experiences when you were surprised by an individual's or group's capacity.

- You may have been taken completely by surprise—you didn't know they had it in them.
- Perhaps you thought they had some level of skill but then they demonstrated far more skill than you expected.
- Perhaps they resolved a tough issue in surprisingly creative ways.
- Perhaps you felt humbled by their depth of commitment and willingness to stay with the issue/task/challenge until it was resolved.
- Perhaps there were other ways people surprised you.

Bring these experiences into your awareness with as much vividness as possible. Recall specific people or moments that stand out for you even now. What's your most recent experience of being surprised?

From this recall, how would you describe the human spirit you witnessed and possibly benefited from? What qualities and capacities do we humans possess? What were the conditions or circumstances that evoked these qualities?

How strong is your confidence that people can be generous, creative, and kind?

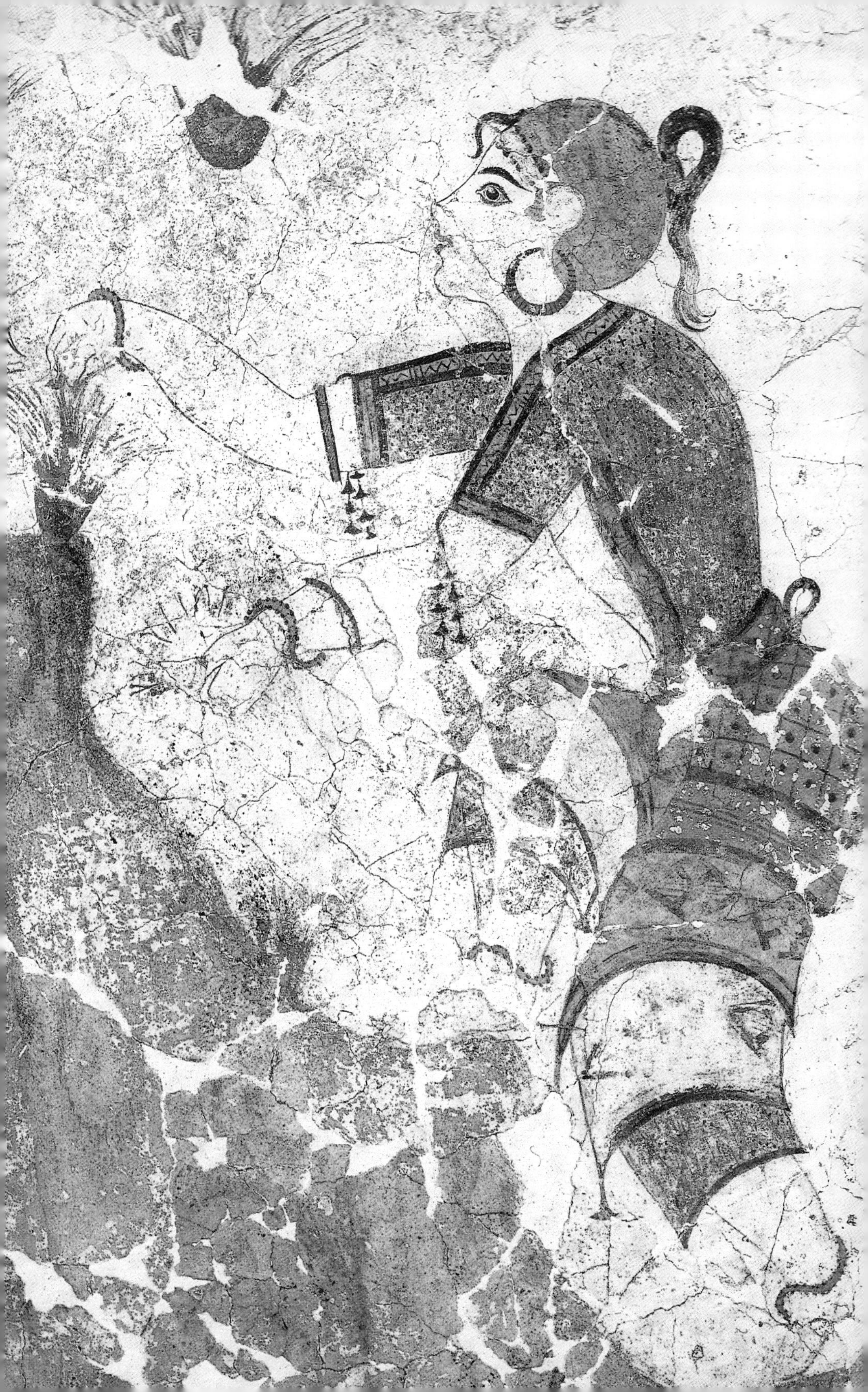

16

Becoming an Island of Sanity

An Island of Sanity is a gift of possibility and refuge. It sets itself apart from the destructive dynamics, policies, and behaviors that are afflicting people on the mainland. It needs to be an island because there is no other way to preserve and protect our best human qualities. We are not seeking sanctuary—we are seeking contribution. We are magnetized by the island's offerings—the possibility of working together in harmonious relationships to accomplish meaningful work.

Refugia (reh-FYU-jee-ah) is a biological term describing places of shelter where life endures in times of crisis, such as a volcanic eruption, fire, or stressed climate. Ideally, these refugia endure, expand, and connect so that new life emerges.

- Who Do You Invite onto Your Island?
- Creating Coherence at the Core: The Power of Identity
- Do We Need to Be an Island?
- Do We Share a Faith in People?
- Keeping Identity Alive and Well

Who Do You Invite onto Your Island?

Islands of Sanity are not geographic islands. They're created by people who realize they can't continue to do meaningful work without the support and protection offered by an island identity. Many people seek support from networks, interest groups, or communities of practice. This has been going on for decades, and today people are more anxiously seeking community. People join multiple networks, online summits, conferences, one-time gatherings, support groups, book clubs, and other means to affiliate with like-minded others.

But an island is a different order of community requiring a different depth of commitment. We commit to being there for one another, to keep the health of the community paramount. We need a strong community to focus on our work to awaken people's innate and great qualities of generosity, creativity, and kindness. We are not there for ourselves—we do the difficult work of staying healthy as a community so we can do the wonderful work of serving the human spirit.

Who should you invite onto your island? Anyone who's willing to join. Perhaps they're people within the organization, perhaps they're people within your networks, perhaps they're people within your geographic area. You put out the invitation and see who shows up. These first practices use both individual and group inquiry to explore personal motivation, the need to be an island, and the commitment to begin creating our Island of Sanity.

Creating Coherence at the Core: The Power of Identity

The first act of life is to create an identity, a membrane or boundary that distinguishes something from everything else. Without identity, there is no way to differentiate one thing from another or to decide what's needed and what's not. Without identity, life is a messy primordial soup devoid of form and possibility. Some level of exclusion is essential to develop complexity and order. Once a boundary defines what's in and what's out, what's inside starts working together instead of trying to relate to everything and everybody. However, the identity boundary must be semipermeable, in continual exchanges with its environment. Without permeability, without inputs of energy and newness, living systems wear out and die. Organizations become rigid and implode from their own weight. Yet with too much permeability, there's no sensemaking capacity. Organizations try too many things and wear down from a lack of resources and focus.

An Island of Sanity has a clear boundary to protect it from the external environment that prohibits possibilities. Without that boundary, everyone remains vulnerable to the dynamics that are causing so much destruction. Yet the boundary is semipermeable so that adaptation can continue. As an island, people need to stay alert to what's happening beyond their shores, adapt as needed, and ensure that every response strengthens community.

In organizations and communities, identity plays the critical role in creating order for free. Instead of rules and policies to define and regulate behaviors, a strong identity creates coherence at the core. This identity must be known and valued by everyone. We don't need rule manuals when we know who we are, what we value, and how we act. We see these values and behaviors practiced throughout the organization. We have confidence that they are real.

This coherence, this integrity, empowers individuals to make their own decisions and determine their actions. This is self-organization, using a self (shared identity) to organize responses and define the work.

In a community that identifies itself as an Island of Sanity, we recognize that to do work that evokes people's best qualities, we need to separate ourselves as best we can from the overpowering and destructive dynamics of this time. We realize we cannot be who we want to be or do what we aspire to do if we remain isolated individuals swimming in the toxic seas. We have a strong desire to serve this time and to stay engaged, and we know we cannot do this alone. We must withdraw psychically and spiritually and create this identity: a devoted community creating the conditions of possibility and sanctuary in order to do the good work of serving the human spirit.

Practice
Do We Need to Be an Island?

Why do this: This first gathering of potential island members is a discovery and formation process. At the end of this process, people decide whether they are willing to commit to the first stage of creating an island identity. It's an experiment—until we start working together, we have no idea of what it requires. This first conversation is essential—it creates the conditions for people to join together to discover what it takes to form as an Island of Sanity.

How to do this: Schedule a gathering (in person or online) minimally for two hours. Invite everyone who expressed interest in the idea of an Island of Sanity. Distribute the questions for personal contemplation a few days ahead of your meeting. Encourage people to reflect on these. Their personal reflections will be shared at the gathering.

Once together, go through the questions in sequence as described below. Don't rush through any stage, and don't allow anyone to highjack the meeting with their personal needs or dramas.

Questions for Personal Contemplation

1. Name a challenge, dilemma, or event where you withdrew rather than joined. Why did you withdraw? There may be several, but choose just one or two.

2. How often do you question whether you can continue to do your work, even work that is meaningful to you?

3. Do you want to stay engaged and find ways to meaningfully contribute to this time?

4. Can you envision yourself as a member of a community that consciously sets itself apart from current culture's destructive dynamics? Do you understand the need for this to be an island?

5. It's easy to fantasize about being part of such a great community, but creating a healthy community demands very hard work and long-term commitment. You won't know what this means until you've joined, but at this point can you commit to taking the first steps to create this Island of Sanity?

Group Conversations Sequence

First: Begin with questions 1–3. These questions are very personal. They illuminate how we each experience current culture by asking: How am I doing? Am I still motivated to contribute? Listen for what's common and also unique. This first conversation gives people a chance to learn who's here as well as to present themselves.

Second: Reflect together on question 4. Sometimes people resist the need to be an island, especially if they're sensitive to the needs for inclusion. Explore this in detail. Refer to the description of the functions of boundaries as was just described in Chapter 16 (Creating Coherence at the Core).

Third: Question 5 asks that people commit to the first steps of forming community. People need to experience working together, so this is just the first experiment. The quality of this first inquiry—how it felt to be together—will play a significant role in their decision. People may ask for more time to decide, which is appropriate. Confirm a date when they'll give you their decision.

After the "Starter Island" group forms, here's the first agreement: for those who commit to starting, ask that they agree to come for three more gatherings. People need to know that each of us is willing to give it time, that people won't suddenly disappear. None of the behaviors common in this internet age of scrolling, clicking, likes, and don't likes will work in creating a group of people who learn to depend on one another. So this first agreement is essential.

Whenever you have an identified group, schedule the next gathering to explore your shared faith and get to know one another better. After that session, design subsequent sessions to deepen relationships and perhaps identify a project they want to work on together. (But don't rush into action, as people may want to do.) There are many processes for creating a healthy group; use the pattern language to choose from the wealth of processes.

Practice
Do We Share a Faith in People?

Why do this: Communities who share a faith are much more likely to persevere through the predictable and unavoidable challenges of being in community. This practice explores whether our individual faith in people coalesces into a shared faith in the human spirit. Subsequent practices will also deepen and strengthen this essential faith.

How to do this: This exploration works in the moment, without any prior reflections. In circle, ask everyone to recall a story or two and to share them. Everyone listens without comment or interference. Ensure that everyone contributes.

1. Recall a few stories that made you aware of people's astonishing capacities to be generous, creative, and kind. Listen well as each shares their stories.

2. From these stories, what generalizations can be made about people at their best? Can you name specific qualities that give people the capacity to stay together? To find meaning? To create? To persevere?

3. As you continue to reflect together, determine whether your faith in the human spirit is shared. Is this faith strong enough for us to begin the hard and blessed work of becoming an Island of Sanity?

Many years ago, the Dalai Lama asked
a group of professionals
(including friends who told me this story)
"What is the cause of suffering?"
Everybody had an answer:
Poverty. Injustice. War. Alienation. Racism.
After listening to their answers,
he abruptly interrupted them.
No, he said,
the cause of suffering is
when good people begin
their work together
and then fail to notice
what is arising
between them.

Practice
Keeping Identity Alive and Well

Periodically, as we develop experience in being together, doing our work together and apart, it's essential to take time to reflect together on the strength of our island identity. With the pace of change, I recommend doing this quarterly as a half-day formal reflection process.

- What are we learning about being an island?
- Is our commitment to stay together strengthening or weakening?
- Where has our faith in people been challenged? Where has it been strengthened? (Share stories.)
- What have I learned that I want to share with the community? (Everyone offers personal lessons learned.)
- How can we better support one another?
- What is arising between us that we should notice?

17

A Pattern Language to Awaken Generosity, Creativity, and Kindness

A pattern language takes its instructions from life. The patterns are not created by human intelligence. We observe what brings forth the order and harmony inherent in life. We learn what evokes and supports people's innate yearnings to be in good relationships, to learn and contribute in meaningful ways, to develop their skills and talents, and to persevere.

- What Is a Pattern Language?
- A Pattern Language to Engage Our Human Spirits
- Design Principles

What Is a Pattern Language?

Christopher Alexander was an extraordinary British and American architect who gifted us with the concept of "pattern language." He created a language of design that he named "a timeless way of building." This language codified the forms and patterns of design that create timeless beauty and belonging, what we experience in ancient villages or an African rondavel that the land embraces. He did not invent these patterns; he discerned them through intimate observations and experimentation. Alexander worked reverentially with the natural order of life—inside his buildings you feel welcomed by their beauty, harmony, and scale.

Friends and I worked with his concepts for many years to develop pattern languages for human interactions in the workplace. It was quite a challenge inside massive concrete towers and endless corridors of power designed to make people feel small and insignificant. But even so, we learned what evokes our human spirits, the forms and processes that work even in suffocating environments. We each expressed our learnings in different ways. Here is my pattern language distilled from many years of working globally, always astonished at what's possible when people care about their work and commit to staying together even in the most difficult conditions.

A pattern language takes its instructions from life. The patterns are intrinsic, discerned but not created by human intelligence. As keen observers and bold experimenters, we learn what brings forth the order and harmony inherent in life. As leaders and facilitators, we learn what evokes and supports people's constant yearnings to be in good relationships, to learn and contribute in meaningful ways, to develop their skills and talents, and to have the will to persevere. These yearnings are fundamental in all people. With the right processes and devoted leadership, people can fulfill their longings in ways that are generous, creative, and kind.

A pattern language works in intimate partnership with life's dynamics rather than our invented process designs. Working with life, working with the human spirit, we are assured of success.

The Beauty Way of Navajo (Diné) people is a pattern language. It is not an aesthetic. It is recognizing, honoring, and partnering with life through ritual, prayer, and ways of being to evoke life's order, harmony, and balance. This is beauty—and it is everywhere. A Navajo grandmother challenged her granddaughter as they welcomed the dawn, "Find me something not beautiful. It's all beautiful."

A Pattern Language to Engage Our Human Spirits

Where are we with attempts to create more harmonious and productive relationships through diversity, equity, and inclusion efforts? We had strong intentions to value differences, to put an end to years of exclusion and separation, to create equity and justice as norms, not policies. We wanted to undo and repair, to make amends and heal this time of oppressive and fractured relationships. But now we experience the opposite of what we intended—more separation and resentment, more distrust and conflict, more withdrawal and fear of the other.

Although the number is quickly decreasing, there are still communities and organizations where it is possible to engage collectively in creating possibilities and solving problems. Nearly all humans want to contribute to finding solutions to what affects or afflicts them. With sane leadership, there is the possibility of reviving human spirits to work well together. It requires genuine curiosity about one another and perseverance to stay and not withdraw. Practices must be carefully structured to bring people together in meaningful and productive ways with fewer unintended consequences, practices that awaken generosity, creativity, and kindness.

As sane leaders, our commitment is to bring people together in ways that evoke our best human qualities. These qualities reside in our human spirits, not our separate identities. When we bring people together, we are not interested in assembling categories of difference. We create conditions that depend upon difference—perspectives and insights unique to each person because of who they are, what they've experienced, what they care about. These yearnings and capacities cannot be defined by categories of identity. They come to light as we work together. They are valued as we discover how creative we can be together.

Here is a pattern language to create these conditions. These are design principles that work with basic human longings. Today, there is a wealth of good processes designed to empower, engage, create, solve, and develop healthy interactions, healthy conversations, and healthy communities. Use the design principles of this pattern language to select from the abundance of processes that support people working well together.

As design principles, these provide the basic architecture for people working on something important for their team, organization, or community. As architectural rules, they take many different forms but always with the same result. It will be far easier for people to be generous, creative, and kind.

I remember well one of Christopher Alexander's design principles about natural light in a room. If there are windows on two different walls, the space will feel more spacious and brighter than with just one window, even if it's very large. Light from multiple sources always creates greater luminosity.

Design Principles

Diversity: *Complex issues demand difference to find solutions.*
Complex problems (what's not complex these days?) require multiple perspectives. Complexity only comes into focus from many unique perceptions. To understand an issue, crisis, or complex problem, difference maximizes understanding. No single person, expert, or group sees sufficiently. We each see the world differently—real solutions emerge when we honor this fact.

Inclusion: *People need to feel needed.*
"Necessity is the mother of invention." It is also the Mother of Inclusion. Who needs to be here? If they're absent, what information will be lost? The work defines who needs to be here. To fully understand and resolve the issue, we need to include everyone who's played a role or has been affected by this. When people are invited, they need to know that they're necessary; this work can't be done without them.

Equality: *Begin and end as equals.*
We never know whose contribution will be essential. The form of meeting must assert equality. Circle is the form of equality. Use it when everyone's voice is necessary, when power dynamics need to be equalized, when a person's culture inhibits their participation. Always start and end in circle. But it's not the only form—form follows function. Define what needs to be accomplished and choose the right form for that work. (In Chapter 19, see "Solving Complex Problems" with its deliberate use of different geometric forms.)

The Work: *Place the work in the center and keep it there.*
The issue/problem/crisis/opportunity is why we're here. It is the work, not relationships, that brings us together. As people contribute their perspectives, the issue's complexity expands and deepens. As we absorb its complexity, most people become more curious and engaged. And humbled (experts go quiet). Even though we may feel overwhelmed, we want to stay together; we want to resolve this issue. The work keeps us together. An unusual but predictable consequence of being overwhelmed by complexity is that the group emerges with a clear and relatively simple path forward, a solution nearly everyone can support. This simplicity, the other side of complexity, always feels miraculous.

Motivation: *Strong emotions are to be channeled, not feared.*
People often join out of frustration or anger. But they're here; they haven't withdrawn. They bring energies to work with, not to pacify or dismiss. These have the potential to transform into positive creative energy if people experience others being genuinely curious about their perspective. As their view gets woven into a tapestry of understanding, fiery energies channel themselves into ways to contribute. Everyone would rather be generous, creative, and kind.

Learning: *Learning from experience keeps us alive.*
Everything alive chooses its adaptive responses, how it will continue to survive amid changes in its environment. As I was told when observing the rich learning going on in the U.S. Army's combat training, "It's better to learn than be dead." How strange that in most organizations (and lives) we feel we're too busy to reflect and learn from our experience. For every issue and in every process, times to learn together are essential, not as a casual wish for whenever we have time, but as a commitment to frequent times to learn and reflect. These times are sacrosanct, not to be

For the simplicity on this side of complexity,
I wouldn't give you a fig.
But for the simplicity on the other side of complexity,
for that I would give you anything I have.

Oliver Wendell Holmes Sr.
Physician

Success is not a reward.
Failure is not a punishment.
They're just ordinary parts of life.

Chögyam Trungpa
Buddhist teacher

shortchanged or abandoned. The more intense the crisis, the more often we must meet to reflect and learn.

Experimentation: *Life always gives us feedback.*
Everything is an experiment whether we like it or not. Traditional project planning methods are a setup for failure and consequent blame. Nobody learns anything as everyone rushes for the door. To set up an experiment, determine what you're testing, a hypothesis of cause and effect: if we do this, we expect that. When results contradict your hypothesis, develop a new one. When fueled by curiosity rather than certainty, all facts are friendly. The scientific method is a powerful way to learn from experience. And when there's no fear of blame, people get amazingly creative.

Confidence: *Both success and failure build confidence.*
As people take on issues and challenges important to them, as our human spirits display themselves in useful and wondrous ways, we want to continue; we want to find more opportunities to use our new capacities and new relationships. If our first solutions fail, so what? We'll go back in and try again. And if our first attempts succeed, give us a bigger challenge. People's finest capacities have been awakened and put to good use. Of course they/we want to keep going.

Community: *The well-being of our community supersedes all other concerns.*
Everything in this pattern language contributes to nourishing community. As people feel valued for their contribution, they willingly participate. They now feel part of something beyond themselves and are nurtured by relationships. But things go wrong and relationships fracture. Evaluate every practice for where it directs people's attention: Does it focus on individual needs, or on the community's well-being? Does it strengthen

community or protect individuals? Community must be the first and last concern because its strength or weakness determines success or failure.

Evaluate: *Is this pattern language working?*

As the leader, if you're not seeing these results, look again at these design principles. They work as a whole, so notice which one(s) might have been ignored or overlooked. Approach your discernment with generosity and kindness to yourself—how good that you're experimenting with this! Learn from your experience and try again. And again.

18

From Reactivity to Responsiveness

We cannot see the world. We create our own world and then spend our lives believing it's real and doing everything we can to defend it. Our version of reality isn't true, but it is real for us.

Seeing Clearly to Act Wisely

We all know the familiar maxim "Seeing is believing." But this is not true. Believing is seeing. We can never see reality. We construct our personal version of reality, creating it over a lifetime from our biases, judgments, opinions, cultural imprints, beliefs, and experiences. It cannot be otherwise, but to work well together, we have to realize this fact. We have to commit to learning how to see clearly.

As our seeing expands, it's humbling to realize how little we perceive. Humility makes us curious to discover what else is out there. This is generous and kind perception. We acknowledge our filters and commit to practices to clear our vision. The more curious we are, the more we perceive. As we see more clearly, we often experience surprise and delight. The world is much more interesting and far less threatening as we take the time to see more clearly.

As we open to this world as it is, we feel both joy and sadness—the human experience is right here in our open hearts and minds.

Practice

Seeing the Familiar with New Eyes

Why do this: There are many methods for expanding our perceptions—any of them can create the stark realization of how little we see as we go through our days and lives. Here is a practice to see more of what we thought we knew well. Expect to be surprised and even delighted at what you discover. Curiosity opens us to a world of possibilities, freed of habitual perceptions, judgments, and biases.

How to do this:

a. Practice with a familiar room.

1. Choose a room you know well, e.g. your bedroom, bathroom, or kitchen.

2. Develop the practice of noticing something new every time you walk into this room.

3. Keep doing this as a regular practice—it gets more and more interesting.

b. Practice with your partner, your child, and/or a dear friend.
Every time you're with them, notice something new, something you hadn't noticed before. There's a Buddhist teaching that advises, "If you haven't seen someone for five minutes, don't assume you know them."

c. Practice with someone who's annoying you.

Do the same as with those you love—every time you're with this person, notice something new. See how it affects your attitude or opinion about them.

Taking time to be curious always diminishes our judgments. Our judgments and biases are snapshots we formed over time that then become movies we continually replay in our minds. Curiosity turns the lights on in our mind-theater and dulls the images in the movie. We discover what we never saw before in places, people, and situations. New possibilities and new relationships emerge naturally.

Viktor Frankl, in *Man's Search for Meaning*,
describes the final freedom
that can never be taken from us:
"to choose one's attitude
in any given set of circumstances,
to choose one's own way."

Clearing Our Filters

We want to see clearly in order to act wisely. We want to contribute with sanity, not with emotional outbursts. The space of clear seeing and sane contribution opens wide when we realize how clouded our vision is. We see through our personal filters—no one else sees the world exactly as I do. Our filters develop over time from personal experiences, interpretations, biases, likes and dislikes, culture, and family upbringing. We each see a miniscule bit of reality—an individual grain of sand certain that it understands the ocean, insisting that others agree with its perception.

When we get triggered, we react emotionally to what we think just happened. We've interpreted the situation through our filters. We can't know what really happened but we instantly create a story. It's just our story; it's not reality, but it's very real for us. Once we understand how obscured our vision is, we can become aware rather than reactive. We can use our wonderful human consciousness to become curious about the situation, why we reacted as we did, and what might be a better, more generous response. With self-awareness, we shift from fear to the spacious mind that sees more clearly and can act more wisely.

Practice
The Pause That Refreshes

Why do this: We want to see more clearly. To see more, we have to consciously recognize and clear our filters. The easiest way to see our filters is to notice what triggers us. Once we become aware that we've been triggered, we can choose a different response.

How to do this: Whenever you're triggered in a conversation, situation, or group, follow these steps:

1. Notice you're having a reaction. The body reacts faster than the mind, so notice: Did you tense up? Did your stomach clench, face flush, breathing change, or head hurt? These body signals are early warning signs that you've been triggered. Get to know them. You'll be able to catch yourself sooner, before you get into trouble.

2. Next, change your body posture: sit down, sit up, move back, change rooms, go to the toilet. Shifts in the body shift emotions.

3. Change your gaze: Look for something lovely or interesting. If near a window, look at the sky.

4. Get curious. What triggered you? Was it a phrase, a look, a behavior, a memory?

5. Stay curious. Drop your storyline. Let curiosity calm you down. Open your perceptions to see more.

6. Choose a fresh alternative. How can you respond with generosity and kindness?

7. Take a moment to appreciate yourself. You practiced being responsive rather than reactive.

Practice

When You Can't Let Go

Why do this: We all have times when we can't recover from being triggered. We're angry, upset, and we keep replaying what happened, what that person said or did, how they treated us. We can't let it go; we feel justified in our reaction; we keep obsessing about what they did to us, or what we should have said or done. This can go on for hours, days, even longer. If you want to liberate yourself from this suffocating place, here's a practice to bring fresh air and understanding to this situation.

How to do this: Find a quiet place to support you as you reflect on these questions:

1. ***First reflection:*** Ask yourself (with gentleness), "What did I seem to need in this situation?" You were triggered because you weren't getting some need met. Probe deeply until you feel you've defined what the basic need here is. Name this need(s). If a boundary is one of your needs, define it clearly.

2. ***Second reflection:*** Turn your attention outward, to the other protagonist(s), and ask, "What did they seem to need in this situation?" This is a kind and generous question—you're curious about them rather than only defending yourself.

3. ***Third reflection:*** Look at both sets of needs. Don't discount what you truly need in this situation, but place it in this richer context of needs. With this clarity, choose your response—what might you say and do that can shift this from self-protection and aggression to resolving multiple needs?

4. ***Becoming skilled at noticing your triggers:*** Over time, it gets easier to identify behaviors, comments, and/or people who routinely trigger you. Look for patterns. Once you know your hot buttons, notice how they dissipate just because you've identified them. Strange but true, if you expect to be triggered, chances are you won't be. You'll be able to be with people and in places where your strong reactions had diminished your effectiveness. Now, you can take your seat at tables that formerly provoked and angered you, able to respond and contribute.

19

What Do We Do When Something Goes Wrong?

When things aren't going well, whether it's a sudden crisis or a gradual failure, such moments are filled with information that can save us. "Never waste a good crisis" has been cited by some leaders. However, when a crisis occurs these days, most leaders rush to bury or blame. They rush to find someone to blame or quickly shift focus away from the failure and get on with other things. They want to forget about it as quickly as possible rather than explore it for its life-saving learnings.

Four Practices

Here are four practices that ensure learning from crises and complex problems. They are very different, to be used in different circumstances. But each requires leadership that understands the need for learning, and leaders eager to commit the necessary time and resources.

Each practice succeeds because it engages everyone who was present or affected by what went wrong. Diversity, equity, and inclusion are necessities, not policies or regulations. We need one another to see clearly and act wisely. We need one another to survive and maintain our precious community.

Whatever the Problem, Community Is the Answer

What are the conditions that evoke people's generosity, creativity, and kindness? The answer always is community. It's feeling I belong. It's knowing my contribution is valued. It's being confident that my community can be trusted to depend on inclusion and diversity to solve its issues.

The greatest punishment for humans is exile: physical exile or, today, being canceled, threatened, or hated on social media. Half of Americans report feeling lonely. The British government created a Minister of Loneliness in 2018. This is current culture, and we cannot be surprised at the exponential rise in mental illness and suicide. We need to be together, and when we're isolated by conflict and fear, we literally go crazy.

I assume you experience the costs of isolation and withdrawal in those around you, perhaps in yourself. And many of us have been personally affected by suicide. So we decide to dedicate ourselves to creating a healthy and resilient community as an Island of Sanity.

Yet even as we join together with this strong aspiration, we are still part of this culture that destroys community. We've been conditioned by this culture, we live and work in it, and we still react in ways that harm good relationships. To overcome these relentless negative influences, we dedicate our work to creating healthy community, to use practices that strengthen individuals and community by awakening the human spirit. And still, nourishing healthy community is increasingly more difficult in this culture.

The institute that I cofounded and serve as president, The Berkana Institute, confidently proclaims, "Whatever the problem, community is the answer." Since 1991, we've put this into practice in many different cultures and situations—we know it to be true. But a new depth of meaning in the power of community came from learning about council practices used by Indigenous First Nations in North America.

This Indigenous worldview precept
prioritizes community harmony over punishment or revenge. . . .
[It's] about expanding the circle of blame and benefit
when dealing with hurtful actions.
This is done with the understanding that
the community has played some role
in the injustice or conflict.

Wahinkpe Topa and Darcia Narvaez
in Restoring the Kinship Worldview
(North Atlantic Books, 2022)

Practice
Community Councils

Why do this: Whenever something happens in the community that disrupts or causes harm, that event or individual's behavior is explored as community. Individuals are not singled out for blame and punishment. It's assumed that individual aberrant behavior is a lens for the community—something failed in the community that is reflected in the individual. There are important learnings for the entire community.

These learnings become illuminated using a council inquiry process. The offender sits in the circle as an equal member. There is no debate about inclusion or equality—everyone is necessary if we are to learn from what happened.

How to do this: The process is straightforward and simple. People sit in circle, the form of equality. Everyone is invited to contribute. Each person is listened to with respect and curiosity. No one is blamed or singled out as the cause for what went wrong. (A Lakota Wisdom Keeper told me there's no word for "shame" in his and other Indigenous languages.)

As an island seeking to be a healthy community, we need to pay exquisite attention to relationships. How quickly can we notice when something creates a fissure in relationships, when people become impatient and short-tempered, when our meetings feel tiresome and less productive, when we have less time for one another, when we'd rather be distracted than present?

None of these behaviors may be significant on their own, but each is an early-warning sign that relationships may be weakening. Don't treat them as insignificant; just call a council. Place the health and well-being of the community in the center. Keep it there as the focal point. Whatever issues have arisen, whatever individual behaviors are problematic, explore them as community on behalf of community.

Importantly, all solutions first must benefit the community and then the individual. This may seem harsh because we don't want anyone to feel ignored or excluded. Many times it's possible to serve both community and individuals, but when it's not, community must be the priority. We need to stay together to do our good work. Whatever the problem, community is the answer.

Practice
When Stories Take Hold

Humans are storytellers—it's how we make meaning of anything significant. When we're worried and anxious, we spin our stories even faster, frantic to understand what's happening. (Think of when your child's late coming home, or you hear a rumor of what leaders might be planning.) The greater our anxiety, the more intense our stories—fueled by hot emotions, not cool reason.

When something truly goes wrong in an organization, not rumored but factually true, stories circulate wildly. Everyone is trying to make sense of the situation, fueling their storylines with fear, not awareness.

This is a critical moment for the organization, and it is the leader's role to act as quickly as possible to stop the fear and blame that is fracturing relationships. As a first action, it's common practice for leaders, public relations departments, and commentators to present the facts and to use transparency to dispel rumors and misrepresentations. But in this current culture of distrust and misinformation, facts and explanations most often are twisted to reinforce the validity of the rumor.

How do we stop this story spinning? How do we focus people on facts, not fictions? Here is a process that works well in an Island of Sanity because people are invested in it and want to contribute to its healthy functioning. It can be used in any organization if, and only if, people feel engaged and supportive of the organization. A key aspect of this process is for people to take responsibility for their storylines and acknowledge how these may have intensified the crisis. If they care about the organization, they'll change their behavior. If they don't care, they'll criticize leadership for blaming them and continue to feed on fears and rumors.

Why do this: Use this process when you realize that rumors have taken hold and nothing has worked to stop them. The task is to learn what stories are circulating, name them, and feed them back to the organization for reflection. Once stories are made visible, people are asked to choose which story and what actions they will commit to.

How to do this: **For the leader**

1. ***Choose your intelligence gatherer.*** Determine how you're going to learn what people are saying, what stories are circulating. Who can you trust to be a good listener in places where people congregate? Yes, this is a form of spying, but for a very good purpose. Think of it positively as intelligence gathering to protect the organization. This is what it is.

2. ***Define expectations.*** Set clear boundaries and expectations of the information you want. No names, no positions—you want the narratives, not the narrators. You may want to know which stories have the most strength by functions, departments, or levels.

3. ***Define the stories.*** Once you have the stories and rumors, take time to absorb and make sense of this information. It's best to do this with a few others. Look at all of it from 30,000 feet. Next, name the key narratives—not more than two or three. Hopefully, one story is positive and will stand in contrast to the fear-based one(s). (If there's no positive one, name the two that seem strongest.)

4. ***Gather together.*** After you have defined the core stories, call people together to listen to them. Create hospitable space—comfortable, welcoming, informal. You want people to be open and relaxed, even curious. You're making visible how casual comments, rumors, and fears coalesced into stories that now have their own power and reality. Usually, people are stunned to see what took form from casual comments and exchanges. Give a name to each story—develop each in detail with actual quotes and comments. Feel free to dramatize a bit, especially the absurd parts.

5. ***Present the choice.*** Which story do we want to make true? Which story embodies our values, our aspirations? Which story gives meaning and direction to our continued efforts? If neither story does this, what story do we want to create here and now?

6. ***Keep the names of the stories alive.*** Because the organization has learned from this, the names of the stories can be used as memory joggers. They remind people of how stories develop so easily and how, once visible, they require conscious work to undo.

Where and why this process works: This process works if people care about their work and are committed to the organization. As an Island of Sanity consciously separated from the mainland of fear and misinformation, people are strongly motivated to work with reality. What's truly going on? Why did rumors take hold? This also can be true with teams and organizations if there's a strong learning culture. They too are motivated to learn from the difficulties they encounter and not let fear take over.

Motivated people are intrigued with how fear-based stories develop unconsciously. Once they realize how stories take hold, they become more aware of their own story-generating process. People more quickly distinguish story from fact—it gets easier to stop a story from gathering momentum. This doesn't mean we dismiss everything as "just your story," a phrase that shuts down learning. It means we're committed to distinguishing fact from fiction. We commit to clear thinking to guide our actions. Sane leadership. Clear thinking. Sane actions.

Practice
After Action Reviews

After Action Reviews (AARs) were developed in the United States Army in the 1970s and have since been widely adopted by agencies that deal with crises, such as police, fire, disaster, search and rescue, and other crisis response organizations. Crisis situations demand instant actions under intense pressure using limited information from rapid-fire exchanges. Any break in this chain will determine the outcome. Without question, there is the need to learn from every crisis to ensure fewer failures and more successes in the next crisis.

When the Army initiated the AAR practice, they knew it would be essential to have honest communications among everyone present. It took many years before honesty and a willingness to learn overrode the protocols and expectations of rank. Senior commanders had to listen respectfully to the information coming from the lowest ranks. As AARs were adopted by corporations and governments, they often failed to succeed because power took precedence over learning. It was more important to maintain power and privilege than to learn from experience. Sigh.

I witnessed this process many times while I was working for the then Army Chief of Staff General Gordon R. Sullivan. One of my most memorable experiences was in 1993, observing tank training in the California desert. I witnessed an AAR held at the back of a dusty truck as soldiers tried to understand why they had done so poorly in the maneuvers. Later, having coffee with a colonel, I exclaimed that the Army was the first true learning organization I had been in, even though many corporations claimed that title. He was delighted with the compliment and then explained, "We figured that one out a long time ago. It's better to learn than be dead." Ever since, I have valued and taught this process and used it in my own leadership.

I love this process for what it yields in terms of actionable learnings. Its sole focus is on how to improve performance. I love it because it brings the system together in its diversity of people, roles, and ranks and treats everyone with respect for their contribution. It's the diversity of perceptions that creates genuine insight. And the participatory process of an AAR guarantees that learning will be quickly implemented. People support what they create, and here they are totally involved in determining the learnings, independent of where they sit in the hierarchy. People want to contribute and learn. The AAR process relies on these internal drivers when needed most, at a time of crisis when something's gone wrong.

Core Principles for an AAR

- The process occurs as soon after the event as possible, while the experience is still vivid. Nothing else is more important to do.
- Everyone who was part of the action or crisis is present and expected to contribute.
- Rank and hierarchy don't matter. It is acknowledged that everyone has something of value to contribute. Everyone saw things differently because of where they were.

- The process is disciplined. Specific questions are asked in order. Facilitation is needed to ensure that questions are answered one at a time. Each person speaks without being contradicted or challenged.

- Learnings are recorded in some form. They are available as lessons learned for the benefit of others. This gives additional meaning to the experience—what we just learned might help others.

- Learnings are visible because they are applied immediately. They are not theoretical or filed away for some future time. Learnings change behaviors in the present moment. It's better to learn than be dead.

- People become devoted to this process. Every usage develops the group's capacity and confidence to deal with the next crisis. Seeing the results, people stay engaged, eager to contribute, and confident to take on the next crisis.

The Four Questions of an AAR

How to do this: Ask these one by one in this order. Don't move on to the next question before it's completed. Don't combine them. This requires good facilitation.

1. ***What just happened?*** Each person offers their personal description. No one is challenged on whether their description is accurate. Widely divergent descriptions give the most information and yield the richest understanding. Stay focused on description only. Don't go to question 2 until this is complete.

2. ***Why do you think it happened?*** Each person offers their interpretations, again without being challenged. After everyone has contributed, explore this richness for both diversity and commonalities. Keep probing for differences—these are what build a complete and complex understanding. At the completion of this process, people will have produced a detailed and nuanced narrative that they recognize and can agree on.

   Give this exploration ample time. Beyond the incident, it reveals information about the organization's culture, patterns of communication, expectations, stereotypes, levels of trust, and shared meaning (or not).

3. ***What can we learn from this?*** Here is where the richness of diverse perceptions can be shaped into learning outcomes that build on the complexity of the situation rather than quick simplified analyses. You can rely on the innate motivation of people—we all want to contribute to what we've learned to make our team more effective. We want to help one another.

4. ***How will we apply these learnings?*** Specific actions, defined outcomes, specified work, better communications, and a confident team—all these are possible because of this very fine process.

Practice

Relying on Diversity and Inclusion to Solve Complex Problems

It is increasingly difficult for people to engage with one another at work and in communities. We feel threatened by difference. Threat instantly triggers fear. Our animal brains take over, and we recoil or strike out in self-protection. We blame "them," those others making our lives miserable. We don't want to be near them, much less engage with them. And we're exhausted. So we reject invitations to participate. These behaviors are the new normal in most organizations and communities. Yet even as people withdraw, complex problems keep growing, and the consequences of bad solutions cause increasing harm and suffering.

This process details a structured means for people to come together, explore the complexity of a problem, and together determine solutions. Engaging in this process shifts people's opinions and opposition to creative teamwork. Working together, making good use of difference, they achieve in-depth understanding that then manifests as sane solutions. Such solutions have a higher probability of being implemented—people support what they create. And if/when they encounter difficulty and failure, they'll want to continue experimenting together. People develop confidence that working together creates wiser solutions for what we each care about.

This process works. It engages people in a carefully sequenced order of activities that begins with calming everyone down, then creating space for every perspective to be explained in detail, enriching the problem's complexity. Next the team determines what information, people, and perspectives are missing, what's needed to enrich this problem. They actively search for and invite in more diversity, more information, more people whose perspectives are necessary to fully understand the problem. Diversity and inclusion make this possible, but once engaged, nobody thinks about any other as a category. We're good people, fully engaged, finding solutions for what we all care about.

The final stage is to focus on what needs to be left behind or intentionally removed. This is done with laser-like precision, looking for the minimum that must be compassionately destroyed in order to move forward. People don't like the word destroy, but most organizational changes start with pure destruction, downsizing by 10–20 percent, eliminating programs to reduce costs, firing teams and leaders, reorganizing again and again—practices that only destroy capacity and anger people.

The Five Stages of Solving Complex Problems

These five stages are done in sequence; each stage creates more information and builds relationships. Doing each stage well is critical, but how much time is spent on each depends on the situation and how easy or difficult it is to include more people and get the necessary information. This process is taken from an ancient Tibetan teaching, the Four Karmas or Actions. (Stage five is my recent addition.)

How to Do This

Stage One: *Cooling and Quieting.* Settling people in, becoming good listeners.

Stage Two: *Enriching with Fruitful Opposition.* Exploring differences to gain understanding.

Stage Three: *Magnetizing Resources.* What are we missing? Who else needs to be here?

Stage Four: *Compassionate Destroying.* What needs to be left behind or removed?

Stage Five: *Sane Action.* Implement agreed-upon solutions, using traditional and new planning and implementation processes. Refer to "A Pattern Language to Engage Our Human Spirits" and its "Design Principles."

These five stages are a developmental cycle: one stage creates the conditions for the next. This developmental sequence can sometimes be gone through very quickly, or a group might spend a great deal of time in one stage and move rapidly through the next. Each stage has different core behaviors that facilitate the inquiry for each stage, and each is represented as a geometric form that supports the nature of the inquiry.

The chief cause of problems is solutions.

Eric Sevareid
Newscaster

Stage One: Cooling and Quieting

This first stage relies on an ancient, pacifying form: the circle. The circle is the shape that cools, quiets, pacifies (makes peaceful). It is the form of equality, the most common and enduring form of human meeting. Circles have been found from about 1.5 million years ago (!) as hominids sat around fires to get warm. The equality of the circle was very important—had they sat in any other form, some of them would have frozen.

As soon as you sit in this form, even with a highly conflicted group, people quiet down. Anyone who persists in being dramatic or loud in a circle quickly looks foolish. Circles create inviting space where even those afraid to participate come to feel that their voice is welcome.

The process is straightforward. You go around the circle, and everyone who wants to speak does so in turn and within a limited time period. People who choose not to speak may pass and contribute later. Everyone listens as best they can. People can ask questions for understanding, but no exchanges or debates. The goal is to have each voice heard, for each person to contribute.

Listening yields great benefits. Listening is a reciprocal process: we become better listeners as we are listened to; we become more attentive to others if they have attended to us. The second benefit is that listening brings people together. Watch and you'll see this happening. As people get more engaged, they lean in. The circle becomes tighter. The room gets quieter. The volume decreases while the intensity of listening becomes palpable. As the drama drains, people will still speak passionately, but more quietly and earnestly.

The core behaviors of circle process are patience and curiosity. We are willing to be curious about others' attitudes. And we have to be patient—it takes time to go round a circle and give everyone equal time. If we're impatient, it indicates that we're holding onto our position. We just want to get this over with so we can win using more aggressive approaches. But usually, what's being said by others begins to awaken our curiosity. We learn things we didn't know and develop more awareness of how other people are affected by the problem under consideration.

Stage Two: Enriching with Fruitful Opposition

The form for this second process is a square—we literally want to take sides. We sit in the form of a square if we're physically together, or we hold this mental image. Each person or viewpoint is given time to explain in detail their experience with the issue. Amplifying differences is necessary for our understanding. We listen with respect, not needing to defend our position or demand that we're right.

The intent is to explore the details of difference—only then will we see how complex this problem is. But note that we do this only after we have been together as a circle, settling down, listening to one another, becoming curious.

(We have far too many experiences of public meetings where people stand and scream their views at authorities. Nobody listens, everybody demands time to explain, or yell, and leaders are required to sit there pretending this is a good learning experience for them.)

Each side is responsible for developing their position in depth. This is not the time for sloganeering or campaigning. The task is to go deeply into the rationale and logic of each position. It is important to keep the exploration of each side separate—we are not seeking compromise, blending of views, consensus, or negotiations. Each position has its own logic, and the goal is to develop the unique integrity of each side's position.

As each side presents its perspective, others listen, and soon the inherent complexity of the situation becomes quite evident. Often, people feel overwhelmed as they realize just how complex things really are. But this overwhelm is of great benefit—it moves people off their certainty platform. Confused and overwhelmed, we open to new interpretations and possibilities. Confusion often has a helpful companion, humility. Always, humility is necessary to abandon entrenched positions.

One paradoxical consequence of amplifying differences is that groups emerge feeling more unified. The boundaries of the different positions have lost their hardness, and people begin to talk together as one cohesive group, wanting to resolve the problem together. This feeling of cohesiveness is an essential prerequisite for stage three, noticing what's missing.

Stage Three: Magnetizing Resources

After progressing through the stages of cooling (stage one) and enriching (stage two), it is common for people to feel good about working together as a group, to be humbled by the complexity of the issue, and to be energized to move forward to find solutions. It's a complex array of predictable emotions: people will be both tired and motivated, confused yet confident.

And they'll want to launch into action planning. Actions relieve us of confusion and overwhelm. We are eager to do anything rather than linger longer in these uncomfortable states. However, if actions are planned at this stage, they will be the wrong ones. We do not yet have a sufficient understanding of the issue's complexity to know what actions will be useful. Rushing into actions prematurely ensures unintended consequences, not viable solutions. We need to go deeper into the issue rather than leaping prematurely onto the stage of action.

The form that characterizes the work of stage three is a half circle, a very humbling symbol. It indicates that however far we've come in our understanding of the problem, we're only halfway there. Our comprehension of what's going on is still incomplete, and we need additional perspectives and information to complete the circle of understanding. It can help to sit arrayed along the curve of a half circle, facing out to the blank, incomplete circle. You can put up flip charts or a whiteboard in the empty half of the circle. Or you can draw a circle with one half filled with a summary of your understanding, the other half blank, to be filled in later.

These questions help fill in the blanks:

- What else is there for us to consider?
- What additional information and perspectives do we need?
- Who else needs to be here?
- What are we failing to notice?

The next work for the group is to gather the missing information and invite in those who've been identified as necessary. If we sincerely acknowledge our need for their insights and perspectives, they will be magnetized to join us.

Stage Four: Compassionate Destroying

People often recoil from the word *destroying*. Yet if we look at what's going on in organizations and governments, destroying is the most common response to solving problems. And it's the first response, rather than being the final action after deep and probing exploration of the situation. Too many organizations use weapons of mass destruction rather than smart bombs. They don't know how to act with precision; instead they routinely resort to carpet-bombing. And corporations and governments knowingly take actions and issue policies that destroy people and the planet.

We are focused on letting go, a necessary function in life. Everything has its season, and all things eventually lose their effectiveness and die. We do harm when we hold onto programs and people past their natural life cycles. Realizing when something must be put to rest is a generous and compassionate act.

Stage four comes after deep, thoughtful analysis by a group that has learned how to think well together. At this stage, compassionate destroying is necessary to create capacity for the work ahead. We search for small elements that impede movement forward, to let go of the few things no longer necessary or appropriate for the work we need to do.

To decide what must be compassionately destroyed, we must consider many different things: beliefs, biases, stereotypes; values twisted for personal gain; old practices no longer relevant; habitual dysfunctional behaviors; cultural norms that impede future direction; programs that've outlived their usefulness; policies not working as intended; specific individuals who refuse to change or who block progress.

At this stage, we can be trusted to act with precision and discipline. We are no longer reacting defensively, intent on getting rid of people and things that threaten us. We have a clear picture of the problem and are able to use this clarity to exercise real discernment. We act as compassionate and insightful contributors rather than as excluded or embattled members of the organization or community. We now are skilled enough to discern those small acts of destroying that will yield real benefit.

The form for compassionate destroying is the triangle. A triangle is the most stable structure, sitting on a broad base that supports its apex. The group can sit as a triangle, focused on the apex, working with a flip chart or whiteboard placed at that narrow point. Or people can draw a triangle and focus on the apex area. The core skills of this stage are discipline and discernment. We are restricted by the triangle's apex to select only a small number of things to be eliminated. We apply laser-like discernment to a very complex situation.

This precise discernment is naturally compassionate. We no longer act from self-defense, striking out at what we think harms us. We're clear about those things that impede solutions, those small elements that hold us back or burden us with the past. When we determine what to destroy, we do so from a profound appreciation of the problem.

Stage Five: Sane Action

We are now a cohesive, smart group of people who have developed in-depth perspectives about the problem under consideration. We've included diverse and contrasting views and information in our analysis. We've become good systems thinkers as we've become aware of interconnections and interdependencies. We appreciate the dense interconnections and multiple dynamics at play in this situation.

We've developed skills for working well together. We've become better listeners, become more open and curious, developed new thinking and analytic skills. We've learned to respect those we had misunderstood, ignored, or feared. We've become a more intelligent, diverse, inclusive, and confident team, ready to go to work and experiment with our solutions.

The core behaviors of this stage are commitment and teamwork. We don't need to create them or go off to be trained—they are the result of the work we've done to get this far.

The form for this stage is any and all processes for engagement and teamwork. Now is the time to use the processes that people are familiar with: action learning, strategic thinking, prototyping, project planning, budgeting, measurement. These processes have an important role to play. What's been missing from some of them is sane thinking. Bored or exhausted, people apply them in rote fashion without insight or intelligence. Or they're forced to use them in all situations, even when they make no sense.

Refer to "A Pattern Language to Engage Our Human Spirits" and its "Design Principles." They can infuse these well-worn processes with the light of clear thinking and the energy of strong commitment. Newly developed insights can be used to intelligently determine which actions, measures, and strategies make the most sense. People take responsibility—they will change and discard processes and methods that are dysfunctional or nonsensical.

We have restored sanity, relying on people's generosity, creativity, and kindness.

20

When the Road Gets Hard

- Faith as an Antidote to Fear
- Just Like Me: Using Personal Difficulty to Connect with the Human Experience (*Tonglen*)
- When Your Leadership Is Being Challenged or Attacked
- Put Your Problems in Dwelling Mind
- How to Contemplate
- Meditation Restores Our Sanity

Outsiders will attack you,
and some who follow you,
and at times you will get weary
and turn on each other
from fear and fatigue and
blind forgetfulness.

From "Passover Remembered"
Alla Bozarth-Campbell

Practice
Faith as an Antidote to Fear

In many situations, especially in moments when I'm questioning a decision that resulted in a bad outcome, or when I failed to act wisely, I've used a phrase I learned from leaders of Catholic nuns. For ten years, starting in 2009, the Vatican investigated all U.S. Catholic nuns, accusing them of disobedience, opposition to church doctrine, and lack of faith. This multiyear process at times resembled the Spanish Inquisition. Yet through the series of trials and tribulations, the sisters strengthened their faith, their clarity, and their commitment to serve the poor and forgotten as Jesus had directed. As a witness to their trials with the Vatican, I saw their faith deepen. Each time they encountered opposition, dealt with dismissal and mean-spiritedness, were betrayed and became weary, it was their faith that supported them. And during these years, the faith of all the sisters deepened with prayer and contemplation, showing them the way forward.

Their path of faithfulness was declared early on in a confrontational Vatican meeting when they were challenged by a cardinal who sought to condemn them by noting: "You are not afraid, are you?" One of the sisters voiced what then became their mantra: "We are faithful. Therefore we are not afraid."

This has become my mantra also: "I am faithful. Therefore I am not afraid."

Why do this: When something's gone wrong, when I realize I've truly failed, I begin in the usual ways. I look at the process and decisions that led to my failure. I review key moments and wonder whether I should have said what I said, or reacted as I did. Sometimes I check whether there's anyone I can pin the blame on. Sometimes I harshly condemn myself. Sometimes I want to quit, retire, flee. Always fear is present.

How to do this: For any and all of these reactions, I've learned to go sit quietly in a place that is comfortable and supportive, a place that encourages contemplation. Then I gently ask myself: Have I been faithful? Have I been faithful to the vision that created the intention that took form as actions that harmed or failed? Have I been faithful to this work?

When I contemplate these questions, my fear and lack of confidence disappear. I become far more interested in reaffirming my fidelity than festering in my failure. Of course I will learn from this and try not to repeat mistakes. I will apologize as necessary. But the great gift of this question is that I again know what I am faithful to. I reclaim the ground on which I stand and the faith that nourishes me to serve and keep going.

There's only one need: Do you know what you're faithful to? Have you defined what's of true value, what you stand for, what you will continue to work for even when it becomes hard and disappointing, even when you mess up badly? Is your faith strong enough to dispel fears and failures? Is your faith strengthening you so that, no matter what, you trust yourself to persevere?

Practice

Just Like Me: Using Personal Difficulty to Connect with the Human Experience (*Tonglen*)

Why do this: Here is a simple and oftentimes miraculous practice that transforms our difficult emotional states into deep connections with others, locating self within the human experience. It's a treasured Tibetan Buddhist practice called *tonglen,* "giving and receiving." Tonglen has many forms—in this practice we exchange self with other. We acknowledge our personal suffering and use that awareness to become curious about how many other people, just like me, are feeling the same difficult emotion at this very moment.

How to do this: Find a place that supports you to be quiet and present.

First, notice what you're feeling. Name it. Is it anger, frustration, powerlessness, loneliness, sadness, or another strong feeling? Notice it but don't own it. Don't say "I am angry," but rather say "there is anger." Say this as many times as needed to create a slight distance between you and this feeling. This sounds strange but it works very well. That slight distance between you and the emotion starts to neutralize it. And after all, it's an accurate description of what's going on—an emotion has arisen, but it doesn't define you.

Next get curious. Ask: I wonder how many other people, at this very moment, are experiencing this same feeling? Just like me, how many others are feeling lonely or sad or powerless or ...? Take time to bring specific people, even entire populations, into your awareness. If you're feeling lonely, think of someone you know who may be feeling lonely. Then think of categories of people: the homeless, prisoners, soldiers, migrants, those grieving, those contemplating suicide.

It takes only a second to realize that the world is filled with lonely people. Your experience is common. Nothing special. Nothing to be solved or gotten rid of. At this very moment, probably hundreds of millions of people are having the same experience as you. This recognition is a powerful antidote. You no longer feel like an isolated victim. You're just a normal human being having a painful, common human experience.

With a quiet mind, acknowledge those now in your awareness. Bear witness to their suffering. As they come into your heart, you may find yourself weeping. Send them blessings, prayers, light, wishes that they may find a way out from their suffering.

This practice is tonglen, a Tibetan word for "receiving and sending." With this practice, we use our individual pain to connect with the human experience. The personal is universal; our private suffering transforms into profound connection. Our personal suffering no longer feels as painful or immobilizing. We are not victims but participants. Our compassion may motivate us to find ways to contribute and serve others.

When Your Leadership Is Being Challenged or Attacked

I learned these principles from Catholic sisters, naming them "Leadership Lessons from Besieged Nuns." I witnessed how the leaders of U.S. nuns responded over several years to attempts by the Vatican to condemn, shame, and render them powerless.

When you are challenged, even attacked for your leadership, for your good work, for leading an Island of Sanity, bring these lessons to mind. In the increasingly hateful social media environment, these won't do anything to reduce venomous attacks, but they will serve you well to maintain your mental health and good relationships with your colleagues and community.

Leadership Lessons from Besieged Nuns

1. ***Don't take it personally.*** These attacks targeted at you arise from a larger context. What's going on beyond this moment, what dynamics are at play, what history is coming to fruition, what hateful people have launched the attacks? They might be aiming at you, but really it's not about you.

2. ***Don't play the victim.*** Become aware of all those others, just like me, who are experiencing this same level of abuse, attack, outrage. You're not alone--you're in very good company.

3. ***Avoid all forms of communication except direct conversations.*** Exchanges online distort the message, become more aggressive over time, and threaten even good relationships.

4. ***Find meaning and possibility in the struggle.*** Don't be a martyr, but do keep looking for learnings and experiences that will develop you. They're always present, awaiting your meaning making.

5. ***Define yourself.*** Don't let others define you. You know yourself best. Under attack, it's normal to internalize the accusations and doubt yourself. If you're doubting yourself, ask those who care about you to guide you through this moment, to affirm your skills and qualities, your generosity and kindness.

6. ***Don't abandon yourself or those you love and serve.*** Remember who you are and why you're here. Expect the doubts and lost confidence, but ignore them. Stay focused on your deepest sense of purpose, what you aspire to offer to others.

7. ***Remember your faith, both spiritually and practically.*** Feed your faith: notice times when it nourishes you, when you feel held by it. Notice others' behaviors that confirm your faith.

8. ***Embody your faith.*** Don't talk about it, walk it. People will notice and respond.

9. ***Stay steadfast in your behavior.*** Don't succumb to others' tactics of aggression and fear. There are many examples of when nonviolent behaviors gradually converted violent opposition. Even if you can't change others, you can maintain peace and presence.

Put Your Problems in Dwelling Mind

We use linear mind all the time—in fact, our career success is proof of how well we analyze data, make decisions, measure, and manage. We use linear mind to dissect, to plan, to set timelines and measures. These are important uses of logical thinking. However, logic doesn't work with feelings, intuitions, memories, imagination, and consciousness. The best human qualities cannot be known or measured by rational mind.

Whenever we're stuck on a problem, when linear mind fails to find solutions, when we're frustrated and exhausted without a solution in sight, it's time to contemplate rather than analyze, to take our problems to dwelling mind. (The distinction between dwelling and rational mind was made by the 20th-century German philosopher Martin Heidegger.)

Contemplation is different from meditation. In meditation, we practice to not engage with thoughts, to just watch them come and go. With contemplation, we consciously place a thought, a question, or an idea into our minds and then let the mind play with it. We don't force understanding, we don't analyze, we don't process, we don't make notes. We let our dwelling minds make sense without rational mind's interference.

Contemplation uses the mind differently, more holistically. Once we consciously put a question, problem, phrase, or idea into the space of mind, we let it roam free. Images, memories, concepts, and insights often emerge immediately, but it's important to give mind sufficient time to dwell. We give up the need for instant insight. We relax into contemplation; we trust that our minds are working for us. We discover the feel and taste of this delicious process: it is relaxing, spacious, and fruitful.

Practice
How to Contemplate

1. Find a place that supports you to relax and settle in, free from distraction and noise. Let the space welcome you. If you're in Nature (the best place to be), notice something that's displaying order, harmony, and balance.

2. Do a quick body scan: Notice anywhere in your body that feels tense. Notice it, then move on to the next place. Just notice and keep moving through your body. Don't comment or ask why you're feeling what you're feeling. Let it be. Relax into your seat and the space.

3. Bring whatever you want to contemplate into your mind. Name it, give it some description (as if you're talking to a friend). And then, let go. Don't keep repeating it. Don't obsess about it. Trust your mind to understand. It's got this.

4. Now go do something different. Go for a walk, change locations, notice things around you, get distracted, do a physical activity. Forget about the issue.

5. This process can take hours or days. Be patient. From time to time, gently recall the issue. Don't say too much—just a gentle reminder to your dwelling mind. It's got this.

6. A relaxed and open mind will surprise you with vivid memories from the past. This is normal, but don't get seduced by them. In a few cases, they might be meaningful, but don't get absorbed in them. Don't engage rational mind, don't analyze or wonder why they've come. It's of no benefit to revive them or the emotions they evoke. Acknowledge their appearance, and let them pass.

7. Early on, you may feel you get great insights, even answers. Don't get excited or distracted by them. They're false starts, temptations to stop the process too soon. If they're of real value, you'll remember them.

8. Expect to be surprised. Just when you think nothing good is coming from this process, you might receive an answer or a simple sentence that clarifies everything. We never know when these gifts of insight will appear, but when they do, it's very clear what they are. They feel fresh, new, light, and usually obvious—"Why didn't I think of that sooner?!" You couldn't think of them sooner because you were not in your right mind. You needed dwelling mind.

9. Say thank you. Trust the process. Use it as needed. Frequently.

Meditation Restores Our Sanity

No leader seeking to stay sane and present can get through this time without a structured and regular practice to center, to ground, and to remember how infinitely small yet critically important we are here on Mother Earth.

There are many practices that ground us—gardening, making music, making art, walking the dog, cooking, playing with children—but it is only meditative practice that teaches how to know and manage our minds. As I noted earlier, we make up our own version of reality through identity, personal histories, culture, habitual patterns, beliefs, opinions, preferences. If we want to free ourselves from these mindless influences and choose consciously, we need the capacity to watch our minds, to notice triggers and emotions quickly. This is what meditation practice offers—we become familiar with how we operate. As we learn to meditate, we become good managers of our mental chatter and emotional reactions.

Meditation is badly misunderstood. People try it and exclaim they can't do it because their minds are so busy, always filled with thoughts. Yes, this is true—for all of us. The purpose of meditation is not to get rid of thoughts. It is learning to observe them and not interfere with them, letting them pass by. Eastern spiritual traditions describe mind's purpose: it is to create thoughts. The heart pumps blood, the stomach digests food, the mind produces thoughts. Thoughts come and go endlessly—the mind is just doing its job.

For our work to restore sanity, we need to learn to be present with an opening mind, with minimal triggers, with perception cleared of filters and needs. As we practice meditation, we develop the important muscle of awareness. We learn to be aware of our thoughts and emotions, to notice when they arise, and to not let them control our behavior. We learn to watch thoughts come and go but not get seduced by them.

In meditation, thoughts come and go. They appear and leave on their own if we don't give them life by grasping onto them. They come from nowhere and they return to nowhere. We don't try to get rid of them. We just observe them; we let them be. And as we do, we experience a sense of peace, of heightened awareness, of okayness. Stillness and motion, peacefulness and movement of thoughts—this is the natural state of mind.

Of course, we do get seduced by thoughts while meditating. We're trying to be present but many minutes later realize we've been making lists, telling someone exactly what they should do, dreaming of our next trip or meal, getting lost in a fantasy, or replaying a movie or song. When we notice this, we're awake. Just what we want. Gently, we come back to the breath or our object of meditation. This is the core practice: focus on the breath or object, notice when lost in thought, come back to the breath. Over and over and over. Some days it's easy to stay aware, other days it's impossible. There's no such thing as a good or bad meditation. It's good if you did it, no matter what you experienced.

What I've briefly described is a meditation practice that combines mindfulness with awareness. Mindfulness focuses attention on an object, such as the breath, and awareness teaches us to notice when we've stopped paying attention to that. Combined, this form of meditation practice develops the capacities we need to be awake in the world, to have meditative mind always available.

I offer this practice on my website, and there are many other practices in books and online videos. Find a practice and commit to doing it every day for ten to fifteen minutes. When you realize that you're no longer practicing regularly, come back to it. (We all have these lapses.)

As you practice regularly, you'll notice wonderful and mysterious benefits. Yes, we feel more peaceful and grounded, but we also get things done with greater ease and in less time. Our memory sharpens. We tune in to people better. We have fewer triggers. And we often feel contentment. These are well-established benefits of developing a mind trained to be awake and present. You just have to do it.

Gifts Given and Gifts Received

As we began, I offered this book to you as a gift. If now you are devoted to creating a sanctuary of possibility, an Island of Sanity, you too are offering a gift and will receive many in return. These gifts arise from our heartfelt desire to do all that we can, to learn how to be and how to lead, so that more people experience the strength and beauty of their human spirits. Thank you. Here are just a few of the gifts we offer and receive:

An Island of Sanity is a gift created by generous spirits willing to join together to discover what's possible and who cares.

It is a gift to see each other with new eyes, to discover how eager we are to contribute our generosity, creativity, and kindness.

It is a gift to work together to restore sanity in this insane time. It is brave to open to the world as it is, to listen for what reality is telling us, and to choose our actions based on what is needed.

It is a gift to realize that, just like me, eight billion people want opportunities to contribute, to learn, to be generous, creative, and kind.

The greatest gift we receive is the joy of being together, putting aside petty demands, engaging in work that needs doing, that needs us to be doing it.

We find joy in what we attempted, not in what we accomplished.

We were together. I forget the rest.

“Spring Fresco,” Building Complex Delta, room Delta 2. west wall. Recreated and on display at the National Archaeological Museum of Athens.

All imagery in this book is taken from wall murals discovered on the Greek island of Thera (now Santorini). These rooms were painted during the height of Cycladic culture, somewhere around 2000 BCE. This glorious, deeply Feminine culture was destroyed when the volcano at its center erupted about 1500 BCE. I first discovered this exuberant, joyful, nonhierarchical culture on a trip to Santorini in 2004. I was so moved by these murals that I wrote this poem.

Ancient Thera, Present Teacher
Margaret Wheatley (2004)

The wind working its
way through ancient
cracks and ill-fitting doors pestered
me all night.

Now it is morning and
nothing has settled down the
wind refuses to clear a space
for contemplation. This is stormy

country, lost to fire and sea, buried by meters and
meters of hard pumice rain and heavy boulders,
the volcano falling into its

fiery heart and sea blazing in to fill the steaming
crater that once was island.
Gorgeous culture ended here.

Island home to painters who knew
no restraint who took ceremonial rooms and

made them come alive with color and form
bound by no convention strong
joyful brush strokes bringing

life to barren walls on barren
land their homes painted
still today reminding us of times when

dolphins danced with fleets and
swallows swept the wild sea air
with song. Even now when

it all collapsed and 3500 years of
grief and dust had to be gently cleansed
to see their life even now Theran joy

is here and even now their happy
life lifts my human heart above
my own ruined time and

reminds me that life can be
good even when lived
in the shadow of
what must destroy it.

They knew what was coming.

Many times tremors and ash
warned them to take their
treasures and flee yet they
returned to clean and

rebuild and recreate the life they loved

and then the volcano would
have no more of them and
Earth erupted with violence that
only lives deep inside
creation. All fire the

blast blew black obsidian boulders

like dust, mythic energy reminding
humans how tenderly to walk
the earth that goes from beloved
to fire when it tolerates us

no longer.

Acknowledgments

My life has been richly blessed by wise and caring teachers, true friends, and abundant loving family. For each of you, I am so very grateful and happy that we have journeyed together.

I am grateful for the many people who use my work and experiment with new ways of leading and organizing. I gain strength and enthusiasm from learning of your efforts; it is your endeavors, experimentation, and perseverance that support me. There would be no reason for continuing my own explorations if my work wasn't serving you.

And for our worldwide community of Warriors, may we continue to strengthen one another with our courage, clarity, and devotion to serving others. Whatever the intensity of the outer darkness, may we stay together and grow in wisdom and capacity.

Index

Photo Credits

Dedication: *Ritual with crocus, fresco from Akrotiri, 17th c BC, MPTh, 226322.jpg.* © Zde, September 15, 2022. From Wikimedia Commons.

Part One: *Springtime Fresco with trees, lilies flowers and swallows from palace of Minoan Settlement at Akrotiri on Santorini island, Cyclades, Greece.* © Zzvet, Friday, March 16, 2018. AdobeStock_300425459-2.jpg. From stock.adobe.com.

Part Two: *Wall texture with a relief ornament and painted blue rosettes from Minoan Settlement of Akrotiri on Santorini island, Cyclades, Greece.* © Sunday, March 4, 2018. AdobeStock_306747822.jpeg. From stock.adobe.com.

Page 65: *Saffron gatherer, fresco, Akrotiri, Greece. Cueilleuse de safran, fresque, Akrotiri, Grèce.jpg.* Unknown author. From Wikimedia Commons.

Page 87: *Wall painting of two ladies and papyrus plants from Akrotiri (house of the ladies)* © ArchaiOptix, May 27, 2018. From Wikimedia Commons. *commons.wikimedia.org/wiki/File:Wall_painting_of_two_ladies_and_papyrus_plants_from_Akrotiri_(house_of_the_ladies)_-_Thera_MPT_-_02.jpg.*

Page 134: *Ritual with crocus, fresco from Akrotiri, 17th century BC.* © Zde, September 15, 2022. From Wikimedia Commons. commons.wikimedia.org/wiki/File:Ritual_with_crocus,_fresco_from_Akrotiri,_17th_c_BC,_MPTh,_226321.jpg

Page 140: *Wall painting of two ladies and papyrus plants from Akrotiri (house of the ladies).* © ArchaiOptix, May 27, 2018. From Wikimedia Commons. https://commons.wikimedia.org/wiki/File:Wall_painting_of_two_ladies_and_papyrus_plants_from_Akrotiri_(house_of_the_ladies)_-_Thera_MPT_-_03.jpg

Page 142–143: *Wall painting of spring landscape from Akrotiri (shrine D 2) – Athen NAM - 01.jpg* © ArchaiOptix, October 17, 2014. From Wikimedia Commons.

Margaret J. Wheatley, Ed.D.

Approaching 80, I look back and see what a rich and blessed life I've had. I've been able to give my curiosity free rein and to be with extraordinary teachers and companions. I've been able to explore a wide range of disciplines, lived in several different cultures, and raised a large family.

I've learned from an incredible diversity of people, from Indigenous peoples to the Dalai Lama, from small town ministers to senior government ministers, from leading scientists to National Park rangers, from engaged activists to solitary monastics. This access to so many sources of experience and wisdom, held in the container of friendship, continues to deepen my resolve to bring whatever I'm learning into my books and teachings.

I had an excellent liberal arts education at the University of Rochester and University College London. I served in the Peace Corps in Korea, 1966–1968, learning to thrive in a post-war, traditional culture where everything was different, teaching junior and senior high school English (minimum class size was 65). My M.A. is from New York University in Media Ecology with Neil Postman. My doctorate is from Harvard's program in Administration, Planning, and Social Policy, focused on organizational behavior and change.

I have been a consultant and speaker since 1973, working with all types of organizations and peoples, on all continents (except Antarctica). Working in so many different places, it's been easy to recognize patterns of behavior common across cultural and institutional differences, and to also note behaviors and worldviews specific to different cultures. It also has kept me alert to changing trends in leadership.

I was full-time faculty in two graduate management programs: Cambridge College, Cambridge, Massachusetts, and The Marriott School of Management, Brigham Young University, Provo, Utah. I've been a formal adviser for leadership programs in England, Croatia, Denmark, Australia, and the United States and, with The Berkana Institute, with leadership initiatives in India, Senegal, Zimbabwe, South Africa, Mexico, Brazil, Greece, Canada, and Europe. I was a formal adviser to the director of the National Park System for ten years, a highlight in my career.

I am co-founder and president of The Berkana Institute, a global nonprofit founded in 1991. I am very proud of our decades of experimentation and support of life-affirming leaders everywhere. Explore our rich and varied history at www.berkana.org.

My most creative work is *The Warrior's Songline: A Journey Guided by Voice and Sound* (2020). This is a collaboration with Jerry Granelli. Jerry and I began training Warriors for the Human Spirit in 2015. He was a famous jazz drummer and composer as well as superb teacher of warriorship—he died in 2021, and the Songline is our legacy work. This is a new form melding voice and sound to create an evocative and transcendent experience introducing listeners to the Warrior's path. https://margaretwheatley.com/the-warriors-songline/.

This is my twelfth book, and I've written dozens of articles (free on my website). My writings have been an invitation to explore new ways of leading based on wisdom drawn from new science, history, archeology, cosmology, and many spiritual traditions. I've sought to apply this rich and crucial wisdom to the challenges of leadership and how people can live well together as community, no matter what's happening in external circumstances.

I was raised in the New York City area and then lived in the Boston area. Since 1989, I've lived happily in Utah. I have two adult sons and five stepchildren, all seven from the same father. I have dozens of grandchildren and great-grandchildren, most of whom live in Utah. I am held by the guardian mountains of Utah and frequently seek ground in red rock canyons just a few hours away. My peaceful mountain home supports me to do my work and to take frequent brief spiritual retreats. My spiritual teachers' guidance keeps deepening my spiritual practice, and I delight in the close proximity of beloved family.

To keep current with my work, visit **margaretwheatley.com.**

Berrett–Koehler
Publishers

Berrett-Koehler is an independent publisher dedicated to an ambitious mission: *Connecting people and ideas to create a world that works for all.*

Our publications span many formats, including print, digital, audio, and video. We also offer online resources, training, and gatherings. And we will continue expanding our products and services to advance our mission.

We believe that the solutions to the world's problems will come from all of us, working at all levels: in our society, in our organizations, and in our own lives. Our publications and resources offer pathways to creating a more just, equitable, and sustainable society. They help people make their organizations more humane, democratic, diverse, and effective (and we don't think there's any contradiction there). And they guide people in creating positive change in their own lives and aligning their personal practices with their aspirations for a better world.

And we strive to practice what we preach through what we call "The BK Way." At the core of this approach is *stewardship,* a deep sense of responsibility to administer the company for the benefit of all of our stakeholder groups, including authors, customers, employees, investors, service providers, sales partners, and the communities and environment around us. Everything we do is built around stewardship and our other core values of *quality, partnership, inclusion,* and *sustainability.*

This is why Berrett-Koehler is the first book publishing company to be both a B Corporation (a rigorous certification) and a benefit corporation (a for-profit legal status), which together require us to adhere to the highest standards for corporate, social, and environmental performance. And it is why we have instituted many pioneering practices (which you can learn about at www.bkconnection.com), including the Berrett-Koehler Constitution, the Bill of Rights and Responsibilities for BK Authors, and our unique Author Days.

We are grateful to our readers, authors, and other friends who are supporting our mission. We ask you to share with us examples of how BK publications and resources are making a difference in your lives, organizations, and communities at www.bkconnection.com/impact.

Dear reader,

Thank you for picking up this book and welcome to the worldwide BK community! You're joining a special group of people who have come together to create positive change in their lives, organizations, and communities.

What's BK all about?

Our mission is to connect people and ideas to create a world that works for all.

Why? Our communities, organizations, and lives get bogged down by old paradigms of self-interest, exclusion, hierarchy, and privilege. But we believe that can change. That's why we seek the leading experts on these challenges—and share their actionable ideas with you.

A welcome gift

To help you get started, we'd like to offer you a **free copy** of one of our bestselling ebooks:

www.bkconnection.com/welcome

When you claim your **free ebook**, you'll also be subscribed to our blog.

Our freshest insights

Access the best new tools and ideas for leaders at all levels on our blog at ideas.bkconnection.com.

Sincerely,

Your friends at Berrett-Koehler